Scott French
Paul Van Houten, Ph.D.

•

NEVER SAY LIE

HOW • TO • BEAT
the Machines,
the Interviews,
the Chemical Tests

D1566831

PALADIN PRESS
BOULDER, COLORADO

Also by Scott French:

Credit: The Cutting Edge

High-Tech Harassment: How to Get Even with Anybody, Anytime

SpyGame: Winning Through Super Technology (with Lee Lapin)

Never Say Lie:
How to Beat the Machines, the Interviews, the Chemical Tests
by Scott French and Paul Van Houten, Ph.D.

Copyright © 1987 by Scott French and Paul Van Houten, Ph.D.

ISBN 0-87364-639-8
Printed in the United States of America

Published by Paladin Press, a division of
Paladin Enterprises, Inc., P.O. Box 1307,
Boulder, Colorado 80306, USA.
(303) 443-7250

Direct inquires and/or orders to the above address.

NEVER SAY LIE

HOW TO MISLEAD ANYONE/ANYTHING/ANYTIME-AND GET AWAY WITH IT!!

--BEAT THE HUMANS/KINESIC INTERVIEWING
--BEAT THE MACHINES/LIE DETECTORS-PSE
--BEAT THE PAPER/GRAPHOANALYSIS
--BEAT THE "HONESTY TESTS"
--BEAT THE DRUG TESTS

THE VERY LATEST TECHNIQUES FROM THE FBI, IRS, INTELLIGENCE AGENCIES, POLICE AND PRIVATE SCREENING FIRMS. LEARN TO TELL WHEN ANYONE IS LYING AS WELL AS HOW TO PASS ANY TEST!

NEVER SAY LIE

THE SCIENCE OF MANIPULATING THE TRUTH TELLER. INFORMATION ALIGNMENT THROUGH KNOWLEDGE, DISCIPLINE AND ARTIFICIAL AGENTS...

SCOTT FRENCH
PAUL VAN HOUTEN, Ph.D

Although most of the research for this book was original, a number of specialists, consultants and government researchers contributed in part.

—Thanks to all

TABLE OF CONTENTS

KINESIC INTERVIEWING

A NON-MECHANICAL SYSTEM OF DECEPTION INDICATION

LIES

The first part of our study focuses on a technique known as the Kinesic Interview Technique. This technique, while little known to most of us on the outside world, has been employed for nearly fifteen years by the FBI, extensively by the IRS, many police departments and other interviewers and investigative personnel.

The study of kinesics differs from the use of the polygraph or PSE in the fact that it requires no mechanical device to ascertain truth or levels of stress. Yet it appears to be as accurate as many of these devices if not more so. The study of kinesics has developed by comparing thousands of cases by psychologists, psychoanalysts, polygraph users, cops, and professors.

I have also incorporated a specialist who, as you might guess, prefers to remain anonymous at this time, into my own study of kinesic behavior.

Kinesics is quite accurate. The normal way to study is to take a workshop (average $500 to $1,500). This workshop teaches the interviewer how to control an interview and how to read uncontrolled responses. That is, responses given but unknown by the subject to determine the subject's ability to react to a truthful or untruthful response situation.

Remember we are not just talking about just gut feelings or gut-level reactions on the part of the interviewer or the interviewee. Kinesics actually provides a look at both a person's body and his psychological responses to a statement or set of statements.

As with a polygraph this will indicate extreme stress and will often indicate truth or falsehoods. In reality it makes no difference to most of us whether it is accurate in recording truth or falsehoods because it is going to be taken as accurate by the person doing the interviewing. This means if you are involved in a kinesic interview situation, often unknown to you the subject, your guilt, innocence or even whether you get a job, can be based upon your responses to this particular set of criteria.

Therefore, it follows it is extremely important to realize the nature of a kinesic interview situation--what is read as what and how to beat or condition your responses to achieve the desired results. Chances are several times in your life, especially if you are reading this book, you are going to be faced with a situation in which kinesic interview techniques will be a factor.

There are a number of phases involved in Kinesics. We will go over them here.

The detection phase concentrates on telling guilty people from innocent people through the observation and analysis of their responses. This can be coupled with body position, body language, non-verbal responses and other psychological uncontrolled responses from the subject to determine guilt, innocence or trustworthiness. Every response during an interview situation gives something away. This comes from a subject's childhood and pre-conditioned responses as he grows up. Everyone when faced with a stressful or possibly stressful situation becomes subject to the "run or fight" syndrome. This is a pre-conditioned response that is not consciously thought through by the subject. Yet it can tell a trained observer whether you are under stress, lying or telling the truth.

This situation depends on both responses to an active behavior pattern as well as passive responses. These are uncontrolled responses, often unknown by the subject in question.

Why learn the Kinesic Interview Technique? Simple. You're going to be exposed to this technique whether you apply for a job, are interviewed about stolen money from a cash register, are picked up the FBI because you are an obviously undesirable person, or are questioned by the Internal Revenue Service as to whether your mother-in-law actually did write that book you gave her money for. All kidding aside, this technique is becoming a standard for law enforcement and business personnel. It is important to understand what is going on.

This is especially true when you consider that the average interviewer may not have the facilities or intelligence to correctly interpret or use the Kinesic Interview Technique.

Therefore, it is very possible, even probable, you may lose a job or be considered guilty of a crime or situation you did not commit because of errors on the interviewer's part. Because of this, we are going to teach you how to use the Kinesic Interview Technique as well as how to use it to your benefit.

As in any other involved technique, it is impossible to read this book once and understand entirely the technique or apply it correctly. Please study this book a number of times, study the pictures and the captions until you understand what is presented and what your reactions should be. Only practice and time will make your reactions natural and flowing as is required to successfully pass a kinesic interview.

Once we have examined the ways in which kinesic interviews can be dealt with naturally, we will also spend some time on defeating or rather passing the interview through mechanical means. A touch of warning, however; using or depending on mechanical means for any important situation is not the way to go. This would be akin to buying a high performance race car and expecting to win a Grand Prix race simply because you have a good car. Unfortunately there is some skill required.

This skill will come from practice and possibly a combination of other techniques. Because this is a rather subtle technique, it requires an expert interviewer to apply correctly. Many are not this expert. Often this technique is not used strictly to find guilt or innocence but rather is employed to speed through an interview. In theory this allows a person interviewing someone for an important job to cut down the time expended to decide if the applicant is, in fact, qualified, truthful, etc., and ready for the position.

These short cuts do not always work. On the other hand, if you know what is going on and can apply our techniques to this interview, you will find in this type of interview, the short cuts work thoroughly to your advantage. You will come out as honest, trustworthy, loyal, helpful, courteous, kind and - well, let's face it - like a Boy Scout

Remember the interviewer is expecting to see unconscious verbal and visual behavior modifications on your part, which will help him understand your emotional state or amount of stress. In theory this provides him the information, the data necessary to get at the truth and decide your qualifications or your guilt or innocence.

He will expect you to exhibit a behavior pattern that indicates your truthfulness or, God forbid, untruthfulness.

A typical kinesic interview is composed of two different setups. The first setup or section is when verbal and/or non-verbal signs are employed to decide your amount of stress or your probability of telling the truth or deception.

Once this is accomplished, a good interviewer will use a second system, which is a setup approach which maximizes the probability of your actually confessing to a crime or slipping and giving away something which will, of course, justify his actions thereafter.

We're going to show you step-by-step how to get by both these phases. Please note: we're not assuming you're guilty. We are assuming you are being approached for an important position or an important part of your life by someone who many not know enough to use this technique correctly. Also, this is not an empirical science. There is no 100% right or wrong method to tell if you're lying, if you're telling the truth, you're trustworthy, you're capable or you're honest. This includes the use of polygraphs, PSE s, kinesic interviews and many other devices employed by government and private agencies around the world.

To depend on such devices as an absolute reflection of a person's honesty or trustworthiness is foolish. Because of that we are simply showing you how to react in order to maximize your positive influence on these types of interviews.

Also, please don't just read this section. Study this section, learn it, and then go on and understand the types of tests used by interrogators with mechanical devices such as the polygraph. You will see many cross-overs, many steps that can be used in both situations.

In order to effectively apply the material we are going to present, from either an interviewer or interviewee's standpoint, one must begin to apply these techniques, body movements, behavior patterns at once in normal everyday situations. You will find this doesn't make you a geek. In fact, if anything, you'll find people respond to you better and feel better about what you are saying.

If you fail to apply these techniques in a normal everyday situation, they will fade from memory and when you suddenly need to call upon these facilities, the well will be dry. Please, think of yourself as an actor or an actress or a great businessman who applies what he has learned in his daily life in order to better himself at his skills. It will pay off.

Remember this book contains a systematic approach to ascertaining truth, guilt or stress reactions and, conversely, producing the reaction wanted in the interrogator. You must read this book a number of times to assimilate all the data correctly. Do it!

Besides applying these techniques to strangers and people in controlled interview situations, learn to listen to yourself and see how many of these clues or situational responses you can detect on your own. In fact, it might be helpful to tape record yourself or if you have access to one, videotape yourself. Analyze your own reactions as you would if you were interrogating yourself.

At this point it is important to realize, in fact, I'll remind you of this several times during this publication that no single response, no single action, no single psychological response is a clear indication of a person's. guilt or innocence. Rather, you must be aware of the synergistic effect of a number of questions or group of responses. Any such group that all tends towards the same analysis will indicate guilt, innocence or stress. One single reaction may simply be a pre-conditioned response to a situation to which you are not aware.

Needless to say, this works both ways. If you find yourself in an interview situation and realize you have just committed a cardinal sin, remember this is only one response. A good interviewer will not judge the entire interview on this response. It's up to you to modify the remainder of your interview to convince the interviewer of what you wish to convince him. A wise man once said, "The difference between a bad athlete and a good athlete is the ability to bounce back." A good tennis player can make a ridiculously stupid shot in front of a national audience and still come back on the next shot with perfection.

In order to become a successful interviewee or, of course, interviewer, you must be able to emulate this type of response. Another way of stating this is you are looking to give or receive a pattern of responses which indicate lying or telling the truth. This pattern is like a woven tapestry. Each thread is only a thread. Yet when seen as a whole the pattern soon emerges. Only after viewing the entire tapestry can one see the the picture. In other words, only after looking at the responses to a variety of questions can one be quite sure of one's conclusions

In order to begin our study of the Kinesic Interview Technique, we're going to start with one one of the most accurate applications of kinesic interviewing. That is what is commonly known as verbal response analysis.

FORMULATED QUESTIONS

Since police work has begun, policemen and their allied counterparts, have noticed that there are certain questions that can be formulated or asked in specific manners that tend to illicit one response if a person is honest and another response if a person is lying.

During the last twenty years a number of psychologists have correlated these questions and the results are used in the Kinesic Interview Technique.   These formulated questions can be thought of as peak of tension questions in a lie detection test or a stress voice analyzer test. They are often woven into the conversation Learn to recognize these questions. Learn to respect these questions and not show undue responses.

For instance, you are at a party where the lights dimmed as in a clue game for five seconds and then the baroness' diamond necklace was gone when the lights came back on. The police are interviewing you as one of the prime suspects because you were a guest mingling with the baroness.

An obvious formulated question is going to be, "Mr. Jones, who do you think had the best chance of stealing the baroness' necklace while the lights were out?"

A typical guilty response is going to be, "Well, you know the servants were everywhere with those little trays full of hors d'oeuvres and I'm almost positive that one of them was looking at the baroness' necklace quite a bit during the party. The man looked unsavory, frankly, and that would be my guess."

That's a lie. The people who had the best chance to steal the necklace were, of course, you and the other guests mingling with the baroness.

A truthful response to that statement would have been, "Actually, I suppose someone with the best chance of stealing the necklace would have been one of the guests who was mingling with the baroness."

In order to use these structured, active questions in the correct sense, certain rules must be observed by the kinesic interviewer. The first and never violated rule is not to throw the question out, not to ask it as a question, but rather to weave it into the conversation as any other part of the interview might have gone. This allows the subconscious behavior of the interviewee to come through without any coloring.

6

In other words, he doesn't have time, or you don't have time in this particular case, to formulate your response, to think about it, your verbal and non-verbal clues are going to be what your body is feeling right then. It also has the effect of panicking you and forcing you into a corner.

Another extremely important rule for a kinesic interviewer is that he never attempts to shape or color the answer he expects from the interviewee. This would be called leading the witness in court and in an interview it tends to discolor the testimony of the witness as well as invalidates the diagnostic response of the actual question. Again a good interviewer will simply ask the question in a straight forward tone with no change of inflection, no special emphasis.

These types of questions should be used in groups. One particular response to one particular question really should not be take as an indication of guilt, although it sometimes is. However, by asking several of these formulated questions, it is possible to ascertain if the interviewer is on the right track and/or has the right person. From there additional non-verbal behavior clues that we'll get into in a moment, can almost always ascertain if the guilt is there.

Before we go any farther, it is also wise to remember that a guilty person will often try and increase the scope of the investigation when asked a question such as the one hypothetical question we just asked, "Who stole the necklace?" Instead of saying, "It was probably one of the four guests who had the best chance, it was probably one of the guests standing next to the baroness, it was probably one of the guests at the party," he's tried to bring in some other section, some other group of people.

He may say, "It could have been one of the guests but I think it was probably one of the servants and you know a mechanic came in to fix the car at one time and he looked very suspicious. Plus there were those caterers. They seemed to leave very rapidly afterwards."

He's tried to broaden the investigation, to thin out the essence of guilt and, of course, thereby to make himself one of the lesser important subjects, if a suspect at all. He's just one of the crowd.

Let's look at some more questions that a good kinesic interviewer will use and get the proper responses.

Now, in our hypothetical situation, we're going to look at another possibility. The person involved here has been accused of a hit and run driving incident. Let's say it's not one where the person was killed, but it is a severe hit and run incident and the police are investigating it.

Another formulated question is and this is asked in a tone that assumes you are not the person, at this point anyway, that they consider the guilty party. "What do you think should happen to somebody like this? That would commit an act like this and leave without telling anyone they were involved in the accident, but just drive off?"

An innocent party will generally go for the "hang 'em high" syndrome. "Go ahead, make my day." In other words the person who had nothing to do with this will usually say, "I think that person should be locked away. That child's leg was broken. He's got traumatic scars on his life. The person who did that does not deserve any mercy in my book."

A person who is guilty will often say, in other words, "Help me."

These words are usually things like, "Well, the person was probably drunk and should be required to see a psychiatrist or attend AA meetings or there should be some investigation into this person's lifestyle. He obviously needs help."

Perhaps the statement could take effect as, "Perhaps the person had personal problems. Maybe he just had a bad fight with his wife. These circumstances should be taken into consideration when you catch the guy, although he should be punished. I think he probably needs help of some sort."

Another time-worn police trick that usually works (in fact this technique is often employed in the good guy-bad guy routine) where the one cop is yelling and maybe grabbing your shirt collar and otherwise coming on in a strong manner while the nice guy is defending you, possibly sending the other cop out into the hall and saying, "You have to excuse him. He once had a daughter involved in a hit and run incident." He is being your friend.

A real formulated question to throw in at this point is to say, "Now, Mr. Jones, is there any reason that one of your neighbors would have to say he actually saw you driving in the vicinity of the accident that night?"

Notice an important fact here. The cop did not say , "One of your neighbors said he saw you there." He simply asked you to give evidence against yourself that there may have been a reason for you to be in that area. No one saw you in that area.

Pay specific attention to these questions. A guilty person will respond, "Well, I did leave to give my grandmother a ride to the Orthodox Church around ten o'clock that night. I suppose I could have been seen going by at that point but I really had nothing to do with the incident in question and I didn't see it happen. I can't be a witness."

An innocent party will respond, "No, there's no reason anyone could have seen me drive by then."

An off-used formulated question is, "Do you think the baroness' necklace was really stolen at the party?"

A guilty person will say one of several options. "No, you want to know the truth, I've heard some rumors about the baroness and her family needing money and it wouldn't surprise me a bit if she'd taken the necklace off, hidden it and is going to claim the insurance on it and resell it to a fence in Switzerland."

Or possibly, "No, that woman is so flighty she probably just mislaid it. I don't even remember seeing the necklace on her. It's going to turn up no doubt in her bedroom someplace, under a pillow. Someone's misplaced the necklace. It's too bad we have to be dragged into this." Those are guilty responses.

An innocent person would say, "I would assume so. The baroness has no reason for lying. That **was** a very valuable necklace and I would imagine she wants to fine it pretty badly."

A good kinesic interviewer will always ask if you are under suspicion, "Has anything like this ever happened to you before?" Obviously the answer here is, "No. It certainly hasn't."

Now if the police have your record and this has happened before, the cop surely will say, "What about April 7, 1967, when you were at another party where a pair of emerald earrings were stolen?"

"Oh, my God, that was fifteen years ago and I didn't realize that's what you meant. Sorry."

You've got nothing to lose by saying no. If you say yes, "I was once accused of stealing a pair of emerald earrings from the King of Sweden's wife, but the investigation later cleared me. They didn't find the earrings."

This implies guilt and normally will be accompanied by other verbal and non-verbal signs during this statement - nervousness, rubbing of hands, sweat, etc.

Note the key word in this is conviction. A truthful subject will say, "No, I haven't been involved in anything like this before." A lying subject will use the word "convicted". "No, I have not been convicted of anything like this before".

Of course there are other formulated response questions which can be asked also, but you get the idea and should be able to pick them out now. Realize that when you are being asked this type of question, the interviewer is on rough ground, thin ice. He doesn't really know where he's going. He's looking for a pattern of guilt, he's looking for a direction to pursue the interview. He's looking for a person who's acting guilty in order to concentrate investigation or other interview techniques on that person.

Answer these responses. Give the correct responses to these questions and you can forestall the investigation in its tracks.

Occasionally an interviewer may use the body strike, the killing blow. In the martial arts the body strike is used to end the fight. This usually takes the effect of, "Well, if you are innocent, why won't you let us search your house?" Especially if the police are knocking on your door.

"Why do we need a warrant to look in your house if you are innocent?" The correct response to this is to throw a body strike back.

"Is this Russia? This is America. I am presumed innocent until proven guilty. My God, I've been to communist countries. Do you know that's how they act in those countries. You people would do better there than you would here. Please go home and read the constitution before you ask me a ridiculous question like that. Thank you."

Hopefully this will throw the interviewer right back on his rear end.

INTERVIEW AND SITUATIONAL CONTROL

Remember in the Kinesic Interview Technique you are learning a response pattern and a way of reading a response pattern that is normally taught to people in aggressive situations. It's even used by sales people trying to close heavy sales - car sales, carpet sales, door-to-door air conditioning sales, all those wonderful things you normally need.

In any interview situation, a good kinesic interviewer tries to utilize the environment to his benefit. That is, he's trying to put you in a stressful situation in order to invoke an uncontrolled response or a confession of guilt. There's a number of ways the interviewer will do this.

The good kinesic interviewer is trying to take your control of the situation away from you. He's trying to make you give up control of your life, and of your thoughts in order to let him take advantage of this lack of control of the space, to move in and manipulate your thought processes. Sounds a little far-fetched? Well, perhaps it is. Perhaps its 1984ish. Perhaps its sort of what they might do in other countries, but--it works and is being used by federal, state, local and private agencies the world over.

In order to examine the interview situation, we are first going to look at it from the standpoint of the interviewer, rather than the interviewee. Kinesic interviewers are taught to control their environment by having the environment in a place which may make you uncomfortable or ill at ease to begin with. Rarely will the FBI ask you to stay at home and they'll come to visit you. No, they'd rather have you come in their office where you may be subjected to long waits, hostile stares from underlings, welcoming gestures that are obviously to make you feel guilty or, in some cases, they may even read you your rights as you walk in the door.

Now this is true whether you're under arrest or not. It is strictly a technique designed to throw you off balance and cause you loss of control or loss of face. You'll often notice that the interviewer has a large, clean desk. He may be in a chair that is larger or taller than your chair. This is common. He's trying to make you feel belittled; he's trying to make you appear to be an underling in this situation.

Always pay close scrutiny to his appearance. He should look extremely powerful. This is generally done by dressing in a suit, a tie, a coat. If there is a badge available, of course, the badge is utilized. He is clean-cut because kinesic interview teaches that beards are distrustful. Beards can indicate guilt or slovenly behavior. No, your interviewer wants to come across as Mr. Clear-blue American. In fact, speaking of the word "blue", kinesic interviewers have discovered the color blue will often make a person feel more at home, more comfortable and, therefore, more likely to talk. You'll notice successful interviewers often wear blue suits. The room itself may be blue to take advantage of this psychological abnormality.

In addition, your interviewer will be very clean-cut. He'll have close-cropped hair, be clean pressed, have scented, minted breath. Oh yes, with that drop of Retsyn for those special situations. All this behavior is intended to make you feel vulnerable, to put you at unease.

Once you are in this situation and the interviewer has established his physical surroundings control, he will attempt to establish a further method of control by violating your zones, your private behavior response zones.

It is interesting to note, every culture has a certain zone of vulnerability. Americans have one, Chinese have another, etc. If you walk down a crowded American street, say Lexington Avenue in New York, it becomes apparent that the people keep a certain distance from each other. This is automatic. It is not because of any real threat. It is simply an implied feeling of comfort. If you walk through the halls of an American prison you will notice a very different zone of behavior because in this case an accidental touch or a bump can be a threatening situation that the other not justified person will react to.

If you walk through Chinatown in any major city or Hong Kong, for instance, you will discover this zone of behavior shrinks. These areas are of a much higher population density and, therefore, by necessity the people have adjusted to much closer physical contact without feeling threatened.

To test your zone of vulnerability, have a friend or someone you trust stand five feet from you. Have him make a fist or hold a rubber knife or in some way effect the possibility of physical violence towards your body. Now have him gradually move closer to you all the time acting out a situation of possible violence. When he reaches a certain level from you, normally arm's length plus a couple inches, you will suddenly feel a different situation, a situation of threat. You will feel if this person was indeed trying to harm you or threaten you, he had just breached your zone of security, making you very vulnerable.

Kinesic interviewers use this same technique to put you at a disadvantage. Like the martial arts, they want you to be on the receiving end, the defensive end where you're much more apt to make a mistake.

Some of the techniques applied by kinesic interviewers are:

Remember, the interviewer will not expect you to confess or react correctly to anyone you do not respect or fear. Therefore, everything he does in the interview situation, is

12

ultimately designed to make you feel one of these emotions.

If the interviewer performs these things correctly, the interviewee will even feel it's his duty to divulge information, true or not. He feels a subconscious urge to please the interviewer, to make himself respected as he respects the interviewer.

A good, experienced interviewer will never show any sign of possible disbelief or possible insecurity. If you sense any of these signs, take advantage of them. Memorize them and realize that your interviewer is nowhere near as strong or successful as he appears to be. Normally, the interviewer will press his advantage. After giving the impression of a clean-cut, powerful all-knowing force, he will lean forward continuing to keep good muscle tone, good facial expression to the point of actually interfering with your zone of comfort. In this way, by leaning forward, by making you feel an almost physical threat, he will force you to react in ways you do not plan to react in. This may cause improper behavior on your part.

To make a long story short, by leaning into your zone of comfort by presenting an image of confidence and all-knowingness, he is making you the vulnerable one. He is making you the victim.

A good kinesic interviewer will be extremely careful of the image he projects. He will not look young and innocent, but he will look clean-cut and powerful. His office will be neat and correct. He will lean into you. He will make you feel respect for him and his questions will appear to indicate respect for you, not as a victim but as a help, as an interviewee who might be able to shed light on the subject. This is a normal situation which causes the interviewee or the victim, depending upon how you look at it, to be forced into a corner, to react to fright during this time, unconsciously or even consciously. Behavior patterns, modifications and verbal clues will then come out unconsciously.

SOME COUNTERMEASURES

As with most exotic technology, as it develops, a field of counter measures also develops, usually just a step or so behind. This is true in weapons, weapon systems, political systems and in this case, polygraph systems.

There are a number of situations, things, devices and procedures that can and do affect the findings of any type of polygraph or stress analysis machine. It is important to note here that I said "any type of stress analysis machine". Most of the techniques we're going into here will also affect the PSE or voice lie detector, voice stress analyzer.

To start off with, begin with some of the lighter and less controllable countermeasures or counterprocedures to the polygraph situation. A number of factors having to do with a person's personality, psychological makeup, physiological makeup and/or intelligence can and often do affect the polygraph readings.

INTELLIGENCE

Intelligence is an additional variable which potentially might affect detectability. The ability of intelligent subjects to anticipate questions may affect polygraph accuracy. One possibility is that intelligent subjects are less detectable because, if trained, they are able to anticipate questions and employ countermeasures. Another possibility is that because intelligent subjects can better understand the implications of a polygraph examination, they will respond to relevant questions with heightened arousal when they are attempting to deceive.

There has been relatively little research on intelligence and polygraph testing. In one of the few experiments which look at intelligence and detectability, Kugelmass found no correlation between intelligence and responsiveness on a peak of tension (POT) card test. On the other hand, research by Gustafson and Orne found that motivation to deceive increased the probability of detection. Barland and Raskin feel this is evidence of the potential role of intelligence. Barland and Raskin's study which compared detection rates among subjects of different education levels, found no difference. However, a separate analysis of the sources of false positive errors by Raskin found that the majority of false positives occurred among subjects who had college degrees.

Subject factors are often described as personality or individual difference factors. They refer to traits associated with individuals that may make them differentially detectable in a polygraph examination. Understanding these effects should enable determination of the conditions under which polygraph testing will yield particular levels of validity. The

14

mechanism by which subject variable affect polygraph examination validity has to do with differential autonomic arousal. Validity is affected when an interaction results between arousal and polygraph testing.

PSYCHOPATHY AND LEVEL OF SOCIALIZATION

One aspect of potential subject effects that has received considerable attention is the effect of level of socialization and psychopathy on detectability. In a series of studies by Waid and his colleagues, significant relationships were found in the laboratory between socialization and autonomic responsiveness. An initial finding was that college students who scored low on socialization (on a standard psychological inventory), gave smaller electrodermal responses (EDRs) to stimuli than did high scoring subjects. In a more directly relevant investigation, a group of college students was asked to deceive or not to deceive a professional polygraph examiner. Results indicated that the subjects who were not detectable were significantly less socialized than those who were detectable. Susceptibility to detection seemed to be mediated by socialization; results indicated that low socialization subjects showed reduced EDRs. Highly socialized subjects were more responsive electrodermally, and as a result, several of them were misclassified as deceptive.

One such experiment:

Procedure:

Thirty male college students (aged 18 to 28 years) participated in an experiment to determine the effect of socialization on detection of deception. The fifteen subjects designated guilty overlearned 6 "code words" during a one hour procedure of time interpolated tasks. The fifteen innocent subjects performed the same tasks but learned no "code words." The experimenters emphasize that care was taken to involve both the innocent and guilty subjects in the task. Guilty subjects were told that highly intelligent, mature individuals could escape detection.

A professional polygraph examiner with no knowledge of a subject's status or the code words administered several types of polygraph tests. The six "code words" differed for the subjects to prevent bias in the examiner. Skin conductance was recorded. The following tests were administered (always in the same order) after a pretest interview to obtain personal history and a review of the relevant questions on the first test: a) Guilty Person Test - Subject was asked three questions about his guilt or innocence and two interpolated control questions. The subject was questioned about his answers, presented a stimulus test, and then a second Guilty Person Test. The first and second Guilty Person Tests differed in that the former used unreviewed control questions, whereas the later reviewed control questions with the subject; b) Peak of Tension Test - Subjects were asked how many correct code words existed. Two series of numbers were presented one with the sequence in ascending order and one with the sequence in descending order; c) Guilty Knowledge Test - Subjects were asked if each of 24 words had special meaning to them. Six of the words were code words. This list was repeated four times.

Subject then completed the socialization scale of the California Psychological Inventory and other questionnaires. Criteria for detection differed with type of test. On the Guilty Person Tests, subjects were classified as deceptive if the response to any of the three critical questions was larger than the largest response to the control questions. Deception was indicated on Peak of Tension if the largest response of the series was to the critical number (omitting the first number). For the Guilty Knowledge test a code word was considered detected if it elicited a larger response than the three code words in the same category. Subjects having code words detected seven or more times were considered deceptive.

There were significant effects for socialization. Deceptive subjects not detected scored significantly lower on the socialization scale than detected deceptives for most of the tests. Among guilty subjects socialization was significantly positively correlated with conductance response magnitude (mean of four tests). Misclassified innocents had higher socialization scores than other innocents. Conductance response magnitude was significantly positively correlated with socialization in innocent subjects. It should be noted that the effectiveness of the different polygraph tests can not be determined in this study, since the tests were administered in the same order for all subjects.

OTHER PSYCHOPATHOLOGY

Guilty psychopaths may escape detection because they are not concerned enough about a misdeed to create interpretable physiological responses. Individuals with other forms of psychopathology may escape detection or be classified as false positives for other reasons (e.g., emotional instability, delusional thinking).

What is different about the psychopath is his attenuated capacity for fearful or guilty apprehension; no psychopath of my acquaintance is deficient in his interest in games, in opportunities to "show off".

There is a theoretical basis for supposing that psychopaths might be more likely to deceive without detection in lie tests, administered under real life conditions, especially if trained to artificially augment their responses to the control questions.

In another place (Lykken, 1976) is a recent case in which a psychopathic prisoner falsely accused a guard of accepting a bribe to smuggle a weapon into the jail. We know now that the prisoner's motive was to have himself transferred to a less secure facility from which he subsequently escaped. Before this matter was conclusively investigated by conventional police methods, both accusor and accused were given standard control-question lie detector tests. The prisoner "passed" and the guard "failed." The guard later described to me his anxiety during the test, how his heart pounded and the sweat dripped, because he knew that his job, his reputation, perhaps even his own freedom might depend upon the outcome. The prisoner, a professional bank robber, had reason for "concern" also since his escape plans hung in the balance, not to mention the possibility of an extension to his sentence. Here is the kind of real life situation in which the psychopath's relative lack of fearful apprehension may give him an advantage in coping with the lie detector.

Guilty or innocent, the normal subject is likely to "fail" the control question lie test, as the evidence confirms. Because he is less disposed toward anxious apprehension, the psychopath might be expected to respond relatively less to the critical questions whether he is innocent or guilty of the real criminal act of which he is suspected. His responses to the "control" questions, too, ought to be relatively attenuated, however, so that the most plausible expectation might be that the psychopath would produce relatively more "inconclusive" outcomes and fewer "deceptive" verdicts than would a normal subject. (If trained to artificially augment his "control" responses, of course, the psychopath should be especially successful in "beating" the lie test.)

KINESIC INTERVIEW TECHNIQUE TRICKS

Many interviews eventually arrive at the truth or at their predestined conclusion. Kinesic interviews are designed to cut through much of the time and obvious effort required to tell if an interviewee is telling the truth or, in some cases, actually get a confession of guilt.

Again we must remind you a good kinesic interviewer practices. He may go to workshops which cost easily $1,000 apiece for the same information available here.

Imagine how easy it would make any interview if you could simply look at a person and know if they were telling the truth or the whole truth and, of course, as we say in the trade, "nothing but the truth". This is what kinesic interview situations are all about. Reading internal preconditioned responses to go beyond the obvious, to go into a person's psyche, to understand a person's id, to understand what a person is doing and saying in reality, not on the surface.

Many times you can talk to someone and feel like he is telling you the truth but not the whole truth or perhaps you can sense intrinsically if a person is lying to you about something. For instance, your mate, let's just say off-handedly, comes up with a story you don't believe is quite true. Even though you're not sure why you don't believe it, you know it isn't true. A good kinesic interviewer will understand, not only if it is true but why it is not.

Remember the kinesic interview is attempting to get information from you or from an interviewee who does not want to give out this information. Therefore, it's up to you to provide the correct environment and correct structure to elicit this information without the subject knowing it or failing that, allowing the subject to want to give you the necessary information.

It is not unusual for a professional interrogator such as the police, the IRS, the FBI, etc., to increase their confession rates 50 to 100% by simply learning and employing the Kinesic Interview Technique. On the other hand, if your an interviewee this represents a 50 to 100% loss.

Let's pay attention to some of the ideas.

The interviewer is going to try to physically control the entire situation. He will do this if done correctly by employing a non-cluttered environment, a desk free of objects you could focus your attention on and thereby eluding his control. He may come out from behind the desk and sit next to you as we have already mentioned in order to invade your sphere of control. How do you counter this? Well, obviously you can't bring your own plants and trees and bushes and pencil sharpeners and set them up on his desk without looking a little suspicious.

One thing you can do is the technique taught by several movie directors. That is known as the "go-to-the-nearest object" technique. When you feel pressured, pushed, cornered, or violent, go to the nearest object. You can get up and move. You can reach over and casually grab the chair or casually touch some object. This is real. This object as it becomes part of your sensory process is real. It is something you can focus your thoughts on and if necessary, take a short period of time to concentrate your thoughts. You can become as concrete as this object.

Failing to have an object to physically go to, find an object in the room that you can look at occasionally if necessary and only during the points of an interview in which it would not indicate lying, which we will get into in just a moment.

Remember, the interviewer is attempting to threaten you. He is attempting to make your body become so stressful that it will react in unconscious manners to relieve that stress. Once the interviewer has established the environment and begun a stressful procedure towards you, he can then easily pick out signs, internal signs on your part as the interviewee, as stress. These signs are symbols of things you grew up with, things that are conditioned in your lifestyle. They are not things that are easy to change and they are things which are apparent to a good interviewer.

The secret here is if you are entirely unaware that these stressful situations are occurring and that you are reacting to them, you're not going to control them. On the other hand, if you become aware of the signs in yourself and in other people of stress and guilt symbols, you can control them.

ACTIVE/PASSIVE BEHAVIOR PATTERNS

There are only two choices in a kinesic interview environment. One is your reactions, you being the interviewee. These are caused by the actions or questions of the interrogator. The other possibility, which is just as bad, is the reactions are coined naturally because of your feelings toward the interview situation. In other words you are unconsciously manifesting your stress outwardly.

Let's look at some items that are definitely considered stressful or meaningful behavior in interview situations. When you're at the peak of a tension question, that is a non-controlled question, any shift in the entire body, in other words crossing the legs, moving the hands, completely shifting from side to side in the chair, is almost always considered a very stressful reaction to this situation or this question. This deals with body positioning after being asked a peak of tension question.

While this shift in position may not indicate guilt, it will tell an interviewer that he is definitely on the right track and is evoking a stressful response in his subject.

There are two obvious countermeasures to this. One is to not shift your body during peak of tension questions, but rather remain with your spirit strong and straightforward. The other is to use a technique often used in the martial arts known as "leading one around by the pillow".   That is to create this tension-indicating bodily shift during a non-peak of tension question or during a time when you are innocent and can prove it. This will mislead the interviewer into an area of non-concern on your part.

Several types of statements during this active/passive phase will indicate stress or even indicate direct guilt. The first is known as an active statement. That is one that the interviewee makes on his own regarding his guilt or the situation without prompting from the interviewer. Granted this may sound silly. No one's going to sit there during the interview and say, "I did it, I did it."

Yet you'd be surprised by the use of judicious timing how it is normal for the average person to want to fill an uncomfortable silence, by talking about the situation, therefore giving something away, letting things slip, or at the very least, exhibiting non-verbal behavior. Be careful of these non-prompted statements. They do you no good whatsoever.

The second type of active/passive behavior is the interviewee's response to structured questions. The questions which are set up by the interviewer to ascertain a certain psychological or physiological response.

The final and often most decisive type of active/passive behavior is entirely passive. That is body language. This can be a shift in your position as we've already mentioned, various hands, legs, arms, nose, chin, signs, movements, lack of movements, stiffness or it can even be changes that are uncontrolled by the interviewee but can be identified by the interviewer in body functions.

In other words, the interviewer is acting almost as a polygraph and gaining important information by your uncontrolled non-activated response patterns. During an interview situation, a kinesic interviewer will consider the fact that everything you do or do not do means something important.

Again it's important to remember a good kinesic interviewer will not regard one response as indicative but will regard a group of movements as conclusive.

Let's look at some active behavior patterns that tend to indicate stress or guilt. The first and most obvious and also the most truthful active behavior pattern is for the interviewee to talk more than he should about the situation. In other words to volunteer information, to give responses to questions that haven't been asked, to explain or to excuse his behavior. Even if he hasn't admitted the behavior is his yet, he can make excuses for some person who would do this sort of thing. This is extremely suspicious.

These types of responses to non-asked questions are definite indications of stressful behavior. It could be likened to being in a fight with someone and seeing them move more than necessary. A good fighter will plant his stance, plan his strategy and act accordingly. Lots of extraneous movement and talk about, "Hey, I got no fight with you, man," indicates nervousness and stress and often means you are not going to win the fight.

Any variation in the speech pattern during a response is a direct sore thumb stick out to a kinesic interviewer. Many times a person will speed his speech up rapidly when denying his guilt or lower his voice at the same time. He may do the opposite. He may slow his speech down to an unnatural level as if trying to convince you, of course, this is true or raise his voice. Both these deviations from the normal baseline, which of course have been established by now by the interviewer, by asking you control questions to see how you respond in normal conversation, are indications of direct stress and/or guilt.

Also cracking of the voice, drying of the lips, licking of the lips, asking for a glass of water, any of these signs are direct indications of subliminal guilt responses by the body, drying up the saliva glands, tightening the throat and exhibiting nervous response to stressful situations.

Two more definite signs are when the mouth of the interviewee moves, especially after answering a question, but he's no longer saying anything. It's obvious his brain is trying to tell him to go on and say something. Maybe something he does not want heard. Any coughing or repeated clearing of the throat is another indication of the person fighting the body's normal reaction to stress. This is generally a good indication of guilt.

How do you counter these situations, especially when you are in the middle of a control situation, and suddenly a peak of tension question is thrown at you? "Isn't the weather nice today, Mr. Jones? We understand you're studying agriculture in school. And by the way, did you steal that money from the cash register?"

The way to get around this, the countermeasure, is the way of strategy. Your spiritual being, your Chi from your stomach, must not be any different from normal. You must practice exhibiting the same tones, same voice pattern, same volume of speech when dealing with stressful situations as when dealing with everyday situations.

You must practice this. Practice with a friend. Practice in stressful situations. Practice in front of an audience. Do not let your body relax. Do not let your spirit slacken. Do not let your spirit be overly calm, but on the other hand, do not allow your body tension to rise. You are simply answering a question the same as you would answer a question about today's weather. Do not think too deeply about the content of the question. Simply concentrate on responding in the same natural flow of events that you have been responding here.

In other words, be neither underspirited or overspirited. Be yourself. You're talking to a friend. Remember you have nothing to fear but "fear itself" - boy, that's a true statement.

It is also important to believe what you are saying. In other words you are not trying to con the enemy, you are not giving him secret little smiles that indicated that "we both know that this is part of a joke". You are cutting the enemy, you are hitting the enemy, you are following through with a natural flow of movement just as if you are trying to convince him of something that is normally very true and very obvious.

KINESIC KEY WORD STRATEGIES

One of the common ways for a person to try and convince another person of his innocence of a situation, is to use the testimonial. The testimonial may be divine, "I swear to God I didn't do this. If God was here, He would tell you."

A testimonial may be to bring in common friends or people in high places or the person's neighbors. "Everyone knows what a great guy I am. If any of those people were here they would tell you that I couldn't have possibly done this."

These testimonials are definite red flags, meaning the person doesn't want to face the question or explain the problems that have led the interviewer to believe his guilt, but rather are attempts to bring in divine testimony to show how he could not possibly be guilty because, after all, he's such a great guy.

This indicates guilt.

Besides these phrases there are a number of key words used in responses which almost always indicate lies. These words are: honestly, frankly, I'm telling you the truth, truthfully, I'm being honest with you here, and of course, the infamous, "If I'm lying may lightning strike me dead. May a truck run through the building and run me over. May my children fall off the cliffs. May ...." and on and on and on. The interviewee does not expect any of these things to happen even though he is lying.

A good kinesic interviewer will not always take one statement of this nature to indicate a complete lie but any group or groupings of these statements, any grouping of these key words, do indicate lies.

"To be completely truthful with you, I didn't burglarize my own house."

Well, chances are you did.

Taking these verbal and non-verbal conclusions that we've discussed so far, the passive and responsive statements and putting them in groupings, you can soon learn to pick out stressful situations and judge truthfulness from lying. Practice.

The way to do this is to spend time during the day listening to your friends, your boss, your wife, your mechanic, your dentist, your doctor. Other people who, of course, always tell you the truth. "No, that knocking sir, means you need a new engine."

In fact, if possible, tape these conversations. Do not tell the people involved you are doing this as it will color their responses and may irritate some of them. Also tape your responses. Tape a day's worth and sit back and listen afterwards. You'll be able to pick out behavior patterns in their responses, their actions as well as your own. The object here is both to learn to use their actions to determine whether they are telling the truth and to shape your actions to indicate the response you want them to indicate.

Practice.

CONTROL SIGNS

One way a successful kinesic interviewer can tell if he has gained control of the situation and therefore is ready to move on to the more meaty part of the interview, is by a technique known as "mirroring." In a mirroring technique the interviewer will deliberately do certain gestures or signs while he is talking to you. Perhaps he rubs his hair, parts his hair in the middle, strokes his hair, rubs his chin slightly while he's talking to you or rubs his neck. He may fold his hands in front of you.

These techniques all imply a distinct movement on his part. They are techniques or movements which are not unusual or weird on the interviewer's part. They are also techniques that would normally not be noticed by an interviewee as anything out of the ordinary. The trick here is the interviewer wants to see you mimic these signs. When he rubs his head and asks you a question or comments upon the weather or that you are probably innocent or whatever technique he is using at the time, his goal is to see you mimic his bodily responses. He is normally not listening at this point to your verbal responses, or if so, is not placing the importance on the verbal response as he is on the mirroring technique of the behavioral response.

When the interviewer is conscious of your mimicking his physical responses, he can assume he has control of the situation and move on to more important, or at least more direct techniques designed to place you in the proverbial uncomfortable position and invoke guilt responses.

Once control has been established by the interviewer, an interesting technique that often produces results is the boredom technique. In this situation the interviewer will apply control questions and peak of tension questions much as used in a polygraph exam except **with the opposite inflections.**

To do this he will appear very interested in what you're saying, perhaps taking notes, maybe recording with your permission, but at least listening very intently to your responses to questions he's asking that are not directly related to the situation at hand. This gives the interviewee a feeling of confidence, a feeling of talking, a feeling of sharing with the interviewer. Of course, if you look at it from an empirical standpoint, he's sharing nothing of value. Nevertheless this induces a behavioral response pattern of sharing information.

When it comes time for the peak of tension type questions, the questions relating directly to the incident or the crux of the matter at hand, the interviewer may pretend boredom. Common ways of doing this are setting the pencil down, rubbing the eyes, looking out the window, dropping the tone and inflections of voice, indicating that he isn't particularly interested in this part of the test, but of course he has to ask the questions because it's part of his job. He will not take notes during this session. He will not stare you in the eyes. He will not act particularly interested.

A good kinesic interviewer will be memorizing or taping this section of the test. Often he will end the test soon afterwards or excuse himself for a while in order to go out and make notes on which you've just said as, of course, this was the peak of tension part of the test. This was the portion that's going to come under direct observation and will determine your eventual test results. Do not be taken in by this.

The obvious countermeasure to this is to simply reverse this situation. You too can act bored, casual and want to share information with your interviewer. Be his buddy. If he's your buddy, all the merrier. Lie or tell the truth whichever is necessary at this point with the correct tonal inflections and with the correct body movements we've covered.

Be aware these are all being recorded either mentally, physically or will soon be recorded after this. If you pull this portion of the test off correctly, you'll find the rest of the test is pretty much down hill because you have probably convinced the interviewer you are telling the truth or responding in the method needed to pass the test.

One way to tell, although it is after the fact normally, that you've been through a boredom peak of tension test, is to notice the interviewer will regain his line of questioning of unimportant information, probably the same line of questioning he was using before entering into the critical phases and will again become very interested in your responses, perhaps writing things down, reasking questions, reestablishing eye contact. Best believe he is writing down what you said two minutes ago not what you're saying right now.

PASSIVE NON-VERBAL RESPONSES TO GUILT

You have seen using the Kinesic Interview Technique approach where the interviewee is pushed into a fight-or-flight syndrome. That is, he is made to feel stress or guilt if there is any underlying cause for the stress or guilt feeling. He is mentally or verbally and sometimes even physically a little bit pushed into a corner.

You've seen how structured questions and structured environments can induce this fight-or-flight syndrome and can help give indication of the subject's guilt or innocence.

Now we are going to take a look at some non-verbal passive response behavior patterns that can almost assuredly indicate guilt. Especially when used in this environment.

The first and perhaps most important technique in the use of passive non-verbal signs is to establish a baseline. Now this same concept is held to be true in all forms of lie detection or stress observation. That is lie detection polygraph tests. You'll find the exact same situation applies.

It is important to know how the interviewee, in this case probably you, reacts to his situation, reacts to the environment and how he reacts to being in a somewhat stressful situation where he's being accused of a crime.

This baseline must be established before any non-verbal behavior signs can be taken as gospel as an indication of guilt. To not do so will often mislead the interviewer entirely. This is important to remember because if you find that through practice you still cannot avoid doing some of these non-verbal guilt indicators, guilt flags, red flags, one way to lessen their impact is to establish them as part of your normal baseline technique during the non-peak of tension or non-critical phases of the test.

By now you should be able to recognize these non-critical phases of the test. Let's say the interviewer is going to discuss the weather with you is an oversimplification, but you should realize when you are going through a non-peak of tension area and, if necessary, establish a rather high baseline or a baseline which includes some of your normal responses to stressful questions. In this way the interviewer is most likely to discount these same responses when they appear in the peak of tension areas during the test.

Remember everyone reacts differently in an interview situation and most people are a little nervous in any sort of interview. Also most people have a pattern of non-verbal responses. That is gestures they will use during a conversation to make a point or during an interview. These are baseline responses. These must be recognized and held non-accountable by the interviewer. Use this to your advantage.

It is possible to invalidate a major portion of this passive non-verbal portion of the test by establishing your baseline or your personality as a person who uses gestures, even nervous-seeming gestures, as a normal part of his conversation.

While it may sound racist, certain types of people, certain races (Mexican or Italian for instance) talk with their hands much more than the average American does. If you appear to fall into one of these categories, you're a type A behavior. You use your hands a lot, you emphasize points with your hands. These same emphasis points will be discounted by a good kinesic interviewer and even a cluster of these same gestures which might indicate guilt in a low baseline situation, will be discounted in a high baseline or, for our purposes, a type A behavior person.

You are now entering a phase which in the martial arts is known as "direct communication" or "body communication". This is the Tao, the true way of the body. In other words, to orally understand this you must teach your body strategies - not your mind - your body. The only way to do this is to practice.

In order to do this and win the situation, you must first learn the approaches used by the interviewer and then absorb the way they are going to be aimed towards you. Then you must practice and become comfortable with the attitude, no attitude response of giving your non-verbal communications to indicate exactly what you want them to indicate.

As I've said one way to do this is to establish a high baseline in the beginning. However, a non-professional kinesic interviewer, may not note the high baseline response and may still interpret these gestures as guilt. It is a far better response to train your body in the method of strategy and to come to know the principle of the Tao, of the way of giving the communication you wish to give with your body.

Obviously the exact opposite of principle applies with regards to your baseline stress level. If you are noticed to be the type of person who does not use gestures, does not punctuate his statements with gestures during the non-peak of tension areas, during the controlled question areas of the test and then suddenly you do use gestures, this is considered a high relative indication of guilt. Watch for this syndrome.

If an interviewee sits very still during the controlled parts of the questions, and even through the tension part of the questions, it will mean one of two things to a good kinesic interviewer: A. The person is feeling very frightened and is sitting very still. This is akin to an animal in the woods listening for a predator. B. The other possibility is that you've read this book or are smart enough to know to sit extremely still and not give away body gestures that indicate guilt.

What does a good kinesic interviewer do in this case? In order to determine which of these responses you are showing, he will then concentrate on smaller, more subtle non-verbal individual body-part movements, which will tell if you are frightened of the interview or are purposely avoiding body movements.

HEAD AND FACE

Most kinesic interviewers believe that the head is by far the most expressive indicator of guilt in any non-verbal situation. Some of the things they watch for are: because stress and guilt usually bring about a change in blood pressure, that is they make one's blood pressure higher, some indications an experienced kinesic interview will look for are indication of increased activity in the carotid artery. The carotid artery can often be observed by the kinesic interviewer and the pulse will appear to throb during high pressure, high tension situations. This is a good indication of guilt.

It is very similar to one of the symptoms picked up by the polygraph machine. One way to avoid this is to practice not allowing this guilt to show, not allowing your artery to produce these movements. Another one is wear a shirt collar that does not show this portion of your neck.

A second very obvious sign is blushing. Most people will look at you and claim, "I never blush. Tell me a dirty joke."

No, maybe a dirty joke does not make you blush but increased blood pressure to the face, which is what causes blushing, is a very normal reaction to guilt or stress. A good kinesic interviewer will watch for this syndrome immediately upon asking a peak of tension question and will often find it.

You must again learn to practice not giving away this sign by not thinking of the question, by having your friends go through these types of questions with you until it becomes normal not to react to them. Or by simply controlling your pulse and your blood pressure through strategy and through this spirit needed to get through a good kinesic interview.

Another sign connected with these two is to watch a person's Adam's apple. When a person is under undue stress and/or lying, the Adam's apple will often bounce up and down, just like in the old Walt Disney movies, and show this condition. Again you must practice avoiding this or wear clothing which covers this portion of your body.

PARRYING THE KINESIC ATTACK

One way often used by guilty parties especially people with some street smarts or people that have had practice at lying, is to not answer an attack. Rather to parry the attack. This again can be likened to a fighting situation where, if someone is attacking with a sword or a knife or a heavy punch, you do not stand in front and directly respond to the attack, rather you spin from it like the wind, you parry the attack.

In most situations this will result in a wind situation because you did not get injured. A good kinesic interviewer will pick up a parry immediately and realize it for what it is. The fact that you don't want to answer a question - then you are probably guilty about that question.

A typical parried response would be if the police took you in and said, "Now tell us, Mr. Smith, did you burglarize your own house, steal the Renoir, collect the insurance and sell it to a fence in Switzerland?"

The obvious response would be to say, "Of course, I didn't. No." Or any logical negative answer.

A parried response would be to say, "Do you really think that I broke into my own house, stole my own painting, collected the insurance on it and then sold it to a fence? Do I seem like that kind of person?"

Well, the obvious responses if you stop to think about it are, "Yes, yes and yes. We think you did that. That's why we're asking you the question."

Do not parry responses in this manner. It will indicate a stressful area if not direct guilt to a good kinesic interviewer. A balanced, strong, spirit-settled, "No. No, I did not. No, I have no idea who did that," is much more convincing than a parry.

Another unusual but sometimes available response from an interviewee here is a Freudian slip. Mr. Smith might say, "Well, yes, I did br----. No, I'm sorry, I didn't mean I burglarized the painting. I meant I did go in the house that night, but, of course, I didn't take the painting. I didn't mean to say that."

This happens more than you would think it does because the inner body, especially one unpracticed in lying, the subconscious id, is trying to tell the truth. A good interviewer will often listen to this first response, the "yes" and disregard the remainder of the response even though it is much longer that says, "No, I didn't. I'm sorry I said that. I really made a mistake there."

Chances are good the first answer was the honest answer. Be careful of this. Practice.

Other indications of parrying a response are to buy time or change the subject by complaining. An interviewee may say, "Do you have to keep it this hot in this building? Don't you realize my time is worth $100 an hour? Do you know what this is costing me? Do you know how far I had to drive to come down here to this building? Couldn't we have had this interview in a more convenient spot or at a more convenient time? Don't you people have anything better to do than harass people like me? Why don't you go out and catch some real crooks?"

These are non-responses. They are non-answers. They are ways of slipping, parrying the question, and hoping that the interviewer will react to the complaint or to the new situation and lose control of the interview. A kinesic interviewer will recognize these responses. Avoid them.

There is an exception to this general rule. If a person appears to cooperate during the interview, which of course, is causing him some discomfort, if not physical at least it is interfering with his normal time schedule, there are places he'd rather be. Now if the interviewee does seem to cooperate with the questions, answers them to the best of his ability, doesn't give off verbal or psychological or body language signs of guilt and then at the end of the interview, does complain about the interview, complain as to being brought down there, complain that it did take a lot of his time, it is often an indication that he has told the truth through the interview.

He was uncomfortable, which of course, is to be expected and in fact, sometimes is encouraged by a kinesic interviewer, yet he didn't want to interrupt the interview. He wanted to ascertain his innocence. He wanted to convince you of his innocence and felt that complaining would distract from that so he waited until the end of the interview to complain about the circumstances. This is normal and may indicate that he is telling the truth . This is a good thing to remember as the interview comes to a close.

An almost dead giveaway to a person's guilt or at least the stress in a situation, is when he comes in to the beginning of the interview and immediately starts complaining. Or even more likely, immediately starts giving reasons and excuses in advance as to why the circumstances don't warrant the obvious conclusions.

This is an attempt on the interviewee's part to dispute what is already on the record or what he is afraid the interviewer is going to ask him. This pre-conditioned response is an obvious area of stress and almost always indicates guilt. The person has been worrying and thinking about what he's going to say and doesn't wait for timing. He's completely out of phase with the interviewer - just wants to make it obvious right off the bat that he's innocent. Well, obviously, he's not.

Any of these excuses given before the interview are simply cover-ups.

INTERVIEWER SEDUCTION

Remember, the interviewer is trying to seduce you, the interviewee, in a manner of speaking. He is trying to get you into bed, he's trying to get you to do something. You've had three drinks and are doing something you might not normally do.

By the same token, it is a common response for the interviewee to try and seduce the interviewer. In other words, it is a very obvious and natural response to tell the IRS man how smart he is, what a beautiful office he has, how you've always wanted to do that yourself. Where did he go to school? By God, you went to school right near there yourself. You don't envy his job, but someone has to do it and you're glad it's someone as honest and caring as he is.

This is bullshit and will stand out directly as such to a kinesic-trained interviewer. This is a sign of guilt, a sign of misleading, a sign of parrying his attack with a weak parry. He will know this.

Another variation of this technique is bonding. Bonding is when a chicken is born from the egg and the first thing he sees he considers "mom". If the first thing he sees is you, you have a chicken following you around for the rest of your life. To over simplify things, this is bonding.

Trying to bond with a professional interviewer, a cop, an IRS man, a FBI man, or a job interviewer is obvious immediately to the interviewer. Do not attempt to find a common ground in the middle of an interview. "Oh, gosh, you drive a Corvette. So do I. You know, I've a suit at home just like that. As a matter of fact, I think we both belong to the Press Club. Haven't I seen you there?" These are obvious bonds and will be read as attempts to parry stress and avoid guilt.

Another signal of extreme stress and very probably guilt is when you, the interviewee, do a dumb thing and say to the interviewer, "This is placing me under stress. I shouldn't be here."

This does not sound logical but think back to times when you have been interviewed or you have been in stressful situations - maybe meeting your girlfriend's father after her rabbit has died. It is not a good sign to say, "This is stressful to me. I have other things to do."

The typical cliche, "Don't you cops have anything better to do than to harass me? Go out and catch some real criminals. I shouldn't be here", is telling the interviewer precisely, "I'm under stress. I feel guilty." Avoid these statements. The interviewer will look for them.

Another dead giveaway, if you excuse the expression, of stress is a change in your attitude of dealing with the interviewer. Perhaps you are on a first name basis. You've begun the interview and he's said "Call me Fred." His name is Fred Smith. Now all of a sudden you've told him about your wife and kids and good old Fred knows this about you and maybe Fred would like to get together sometime and Fred this and Fred that, then comes the peak of tension question. Then Fred becomes Mr. Smith. The interviewer will notice this immediately.

Again, you are varying from your baseline response. You are showing stress and possibly guilt by attempting to formalize the interview from an informal situation. Remember, he's established your baseline as an informal situation up to this point. Of course, the opposite can be true but it is not seen as often. That being the case where it is a formal situation and suddenly you are informal with him. It tends to go the other way and it does indicate stress and often guilt.

NO!!!

In any interview situation the interviewer expects you to deny your guilt, whether you are guilty or not you are going to deny it. Because of this a lot of emphasis is placed on the word "no" itself. When you say no to the crucial or peak of tension questions, the way you say it can determine your guilt or innocence in the kinesic interviewer's eye.

1. Anyone who says no, shifts in his chair, and possibly crosses his legs, is almost always telling a lie.

2. A person who says the word no and then immediately looks in a different direction, out the window, at a point on the wall, is lying.

3. The person who says no and then immediately shuts his eyes afterwards, is lying. He doesn't want to face himself.

4. A person who hesitates and then says no is lying.

5. A person who says no and then shakes his head is probably lying. He's emphasizing something he's already said that there's no reason to emphasize, except of course, to cover a lie.

6. A person who says no breathlessly as though he is amazed you could ask such a thing is lying.

7. A person who says no and then appears to think about what he's just said is probably lying.

8. The syllable "nooooo" stretched over a long time as if it has eight zeros on the end of it, as if you're telling your wife you've neveeeeer thought of cheating on her, is a lie.

9. A no which is qualified by the voice saying it is a lie.

10. A no said as if an apology to something. "I'm sorry I'm saying no", is also a lie.

11. A no said by a look and a pause that indicates that you weren't really talking to him. "Who me, no," is a lie.

12. A no accompanied by eyes that study the interviewer afterwards is a lie.

13. Remember when saying no, the same techniques apply as when answering the rest of the questions. Do not differ from your baseline responses. Keep your spirit the

same. The spirit of a person must remain his mainstay of strategy on the battlefield, in an interview situation or a job interview. Do not qualify your words whether they are the word "no" or whether they are simply conversation.

Remember in kinesic interview counter-strategy it is very important not to effect a loss of balance. You must remain balanced in all portions of the conversation.

Any of these ways of saying no just described show the attack has unbalanced you and you are probably defeated or guilty.

THE EYES HAVE IT

From the time of Sherlock Holmes investigators have known the eyes are the mirror of the soul. The eyes indicate guilt, indicate stress and are reliable measurements of what is going on inside a person. In fact, there is some very sophisticated lie detection gear coming on the market which measures the dilation and the movement of the capillary blood vessels in the eye to give quite a high accuracy in lie detection techniques. The Israelis have used this to pick out tension in persons suspected of being potential terrorists. It has worked for them.

It is possible for a reliable kinesic interviewer to use some of these same signs, these same symbols without expensive machinery. The first and most important rule followed by policemen and investigators everywhere is to look for you to break eye contact with the interviewer.

Next time someone interviews you, even without a professional kinesic background, you'll notice he does this. He'll ask a control question, watch you, and then ask a peak of tension question and watch to see if you break eye contact. He may even leave what feels like a very uncomfortable silence to see if you break contact. Any indication of guilt, any feeling of stress, makes it very normal to break this contact. Obviously you don't want to do this.

A break in eye contact is not always noticed by the interviewer because a good interviewee will break eye contact in various manners, hoping or subconsciously hoping, that this will not be seen as a break in eye contact.

Check our photos and see how some of the different methods of breaking eye contact are used in an interview. Remember a thorough kinesic interviewer will pick up these breaks in eye contact and read them as indications of guilt. Learn to avoid all these movements.

Two of the more mechanical ways of gauging guilt through eye indications are eye pupil constriction. This is the one method used often by the machines and a good kinesic interviewer would practice in being able to pick out the constrictions of one's pupils during an interview.

Another one is rapid eye movement - REM. This unconscious phenomenon (it's one that happens during a specific phase of brain waves, usually during the dreaming stage of sleep) indicates stress or guilt or something else going on in the mind. Ways to avoid this are practice, wear sun glasses which unfortunately does not always work as well as looking somewhat ridiculous, or occasionally take one of a number of drugs which prevent eye constriction by dilating the pupils. The problem with this is that a little too much of the drug or the wrong drug or being subject to an excellent interviewer, may make him very suspicious that you might be on a drug.

Some of the drugs in other parts of this book can possibly be considered to help this phase of the operation.

Two more rather uncontrollable indications of guilt or stress during eye contact interviews are the actual change of color of the eyes. Some people's eyes are much more subject to this than others. The instantaneous change of color after a peak of tension question shows stress or lying.

One thing that can be controlled with practice is the raising of the eye brows. This again is a common indication or stress or guilt and must be overcome.

SANPAKU GUILT

For years macrobiotic people, especially Japanese, have noted a human condition known as Sanpaku . This condition by Americans is called "three whites". It is a condition where three whites of the eye are visible at any one time.

Look in a mirror. Unless you are looking severely upward or severely downward, you should only see white on the left and right of your eye. People who are sanpaku, that is to experience an unbalance in their body are in stressful situation, show three whites in their eye, both sides and the underside of the eye becomes visible.

Historians point out many, many sanpaku people who tended to have met early or violent death or played a hinge part, hinge role in history. Hitler was one. Marilyn Monroe was one. Kennedy was sanpaku - on and on. Did these people lie? Were these people in stressful situations? Yes.

The three whites of the eye concept is a real important indication of stress, guilt and perhaps lying. Look in a mirror. Practice not giving away this sanpaku condition.

Sometimes it is possible to turn the tables on a kinesic interviewer by using a large and broad gauge. This is a two-fold gauge, perception and sight. It is both strong and weak. You are trying to stare down the interviewer rather than being dominated by him, although you do not do this with a violent, mean expression on your face or accompanied with any other signs of guilt. This is strategy.

It is important to see distant things as though they were close and take a distant view of closeness. Your interviewer during this portion of the interview is going to try to take a close look at your eyes and force guilt reactions from your eyes - your pupils, your blood vessels, etc.

It is possible to reverse this by taking a close but non-threatening look at his eyes, staring him down while not breaking eye contact and not violating any of the above rules. You'll be able to sense if you have hit the opponent with this timing correctly and suddenly you will find you are the dominant one in the conversation, not him. Once this has happened, chances of him assessing your guilt correctly has become almost nil.

OTHER HEAD AND FACIAL KINESIC INDICATORS

Kinesic interviewers are taught any contact with the nose or nose area constitutes stress and probably guilt. Watch your friends again. See if this is true. Touching the nose, rubbing the nose, moving the eye glasses up on the nose, attempting to clear invisible particles from the eye by touching the side of the nose, wiping the nose, covering the nose with your hand, covering a sneeze with your hand, are definitely considered very high on the list of factors indicating guilt in any subject in any interview.

Watch it. Practice it. Keep your hands away from your nose.

This can also be used positively. That is, positively from your standpoint during a kinesic interview. Often a person when you are telling him something of interest to him, will tilt his head from one side to the other. This shows he is listening to what you are saying. Afterwards, before he answers, he may hold his head still or perhaps even support his chin with his hand for a moment. This indicates he is thinking about his answer and that he doesn't have a preconceived story to tell. These are good signs. These are signs a kinesic interviewer will take into consideration when determining your stress level or your guilt.

Another factor a kinesic interviewer will look for is the interruption of speech syndrome. That is any time you verbally or unconsciously attempt to interrupt your speech during a peak of tension area of the test.

This is often done by coughing, covering the mouth with the hand even for a second, tightening the lips together, pursing the lips, or running a finger across the lips. Anything that symbolically interrupts the flow of your speech, even though it doesn't interrupt it for more than a split second, should be taken as a sign of guilt and is normally taken that the kinisic interviewer is on the right track. He will pursue this line of questioning.

Also dealing with the mouth, anything that dries the mouth up, cracking of the speech, cracking of the lips, the tongue moistening the lips or asking for a glass of water or a drink is a direct indication of guilt and is always taken as such by any good kinesic interviewer. Try to avoid showing any actions which indicate you are running out of saliva.

The only other possibility associated with the lip movement or licking the lips, is possible attempted seduction of the interviewer. Whether this is physical or mental, interviewees, interviewers of different sexes, and occasionally of the same sex, will try a mental seduction to try to bring the interviewer over to their side. This can often be done and is unconsciously done by oral signs just as in a single's bar. People are concerned with their mouth. They will wet their lips, they will lick their lips.

You have to watch out for these movements. They do not necessarily indicate guilt but are often taken that way. Unless, of course, you pull it off. In which case you are very likely to leave the interviewer with a good feeling about you. Yes, he/she might want to get in your pants, but it's going to be a good feeling. The question of your guilt has now become secondary.

I must advise that this is a rather risky proposition. Unless there are some signs on the interviewer's part, or immediate reactions from your signs, this is not always a wise tact to take.

Even the way a person smiles can be a sign of guilt or stress to a kinesic interviewer, especially if a person has not been smiling and suddenly begins to. An interviewer will look at the smile closely to see if the smile involves the entire mouth as a normal person's smile does or if the smile only shows the upper teeth not the lower. This is a very good single indication of stress, an attempt to take the interviewer in. The interviewee suddenly thinks he has become smarter than the interviewer. Maybe the interviewer has missed some little place or he's backed off on a guilt situation. The smile is an indication of that.

A little off the subject, but a similar indication is when someone forms a pyramid with their hands or fingers between you and him. This is also generally a direct sign he feels superior to the interviewer. He thinks he's smarter than the interviewer, that he's pulled one over on the interviewer. Avoid these situations at all costs.

Either one of these situations normally indicates that the interviewee thinks he has just found his out his escape route. A good kinesic interviewer will go back and look for the flaw or throw any other heavy artillery he has in the battle right then.

THE CHIN

A classic sign of stress and normally guilt is when the interviewee places his fist under his chin as if to support his head and keeps it there, usually nodding or appearing to be thinking, which is what he's doing. This pose is named after the famous sculpture "The Thinker".

Now, obviously, he's not thinking about exactly what the interviewer has asked him, but how to get out of it! He's thinking what he can say, what he has already screwed up, what he can unscrew or what the interviewer already knows about him and he can get around. This posed "The Thinker" is one of the classic guilt indicators in the kinesic interview.

On the other hand, stroking the chin lightly and answering the questions, may be considered a sign of honesty and attempting to answer the questions without thinking too deeply of escape routes.

If the interviewer asks a question and the interviewee immediately at the beginning of the question or at the peak of tension parts of the question, begins to rub his ear or perhaps feel his ear lobe, this is a good indication of stress and possibly guilt.

HEAD AND NECK

An attempt to rub the top of the head, scratch the top of the head or rub the back of the neck as though the muscles are aching somewhat, indicates stress and guilt on the interviewee's part. Especially if the interviewee has appeared not to give guilt cluster signals up to this point, but has appeared to be cooperative.

Now he's having trouble hearing what the interviewer is saying because he doesn't want to hear it. Because it is suddenly striking quite close to home and he wants to avoid it. He's thinking of a way out. He's trying to mentally push the idea out of his mind or off his head.

To carry this one step farther, there is the position where a person clasps or locks his hands behind his neck. This is a very interesting position, which should be read by the kinesic interviewer, as though the person is about to do violence to him. And, yes, he may be about to do violence to him. He has struck home. He has struck gold. He has struck oil. He is very near a confession state or a guilt state.

A good kinesic interviewer will back off at this stage to avoid the violence, but he has gotten the reaction he needed.

It is possible to consider using this gesture to make someone back off a non-critical area. Do not use this gesture during a critical area. Again, this would be leading the man around by the nose, leading him around with the pillow and pointing out guilt in areas where no guilt exists. Do not use violence to emphasize this point as a general rule.

TRUNK AND EXTREMITY KINESIC STRESS INDICATIONS

The rest of the body can also tell much how the interview is progressing and about the guilt or innocence of the subject. One of the first things to notice is the subject, especially during the peak of tension part of the test, leaning toward an exit from the room; say a window, a door, a hallway, even a closet. Is he leaning away from the interviewer noticeably?

This leaning may be his entire body, his shoulder or just his head. Some kinesic interviewers also consider simply pointing the hand towards this exit to mean the same thing. This leaning is a definite symbolic escape mechanism wherein the interviewee is trying to escape from the question because he feels threatened by it and is ready to run.

This is another indication of the fight-or-flight syndrome and he's decided to try flight. This is a definite indication of guilt. Watch yourself. Practice in a mirror. Practice on tape. Practice with friends. Do you lean when you are talking about a sensitive area? Do you think about an exit subconsciously? Do you point toward that exit? If so, you must eliminate this body movement from your repertoire of indications.

Another symbolic movement a good kinesic interviewer will always notice is the crossing movements. When a subject crosses his hands, legs or more likely his arms, in front of himself against the interviewer, he is subconsciously trying to protect his stomach area; again this area of his power base, his Chi, his Tai, from the interviewer.

He is upset with this line of questioning and is attempting to physically protect himself. This does not necessarily indicate guilt. What it does to a good kinesic interviewer is indicate that he must back off, make him relax, make him uncross his arms and legs, in order to open up this reservoir of information the interviewer is seeking.

A good interviewee will not cross his arms or legs during the crucial phase, will remain open and steady as we have constantly hammered on or may again turn this around and use this crossing stage to throw the interviewer off the track by misdirecting the guilt punt.

If instead of leaning or crossing himself, the interviewee turns and exhibits his profile to the interviewer, whether he's facing an exit or not, this is an extremely strong sign of wanting to leave the interview at this point. It is an extremely strong sign of guilt on the question that is being asked at this point and as such read by most good kinesic interviewers.

Similar groups of movements or patterns can be established with other parts of the

41

body, the body extremities in particular. Once a baseline has been established, it is very common to see a person who has been paying attention, been cooperative, suddenly move his hands to his hair and begin grooming his hair or splitting the hair. This is much like rubbing the head. He may return his hands to his body with the elbows held very tightly, perhaps crossed in front of his body after this grooming technique. This is a definite sign of stress and usually a sign of deception.

Another very heavy indication of deception is when the interviewee suddenly, against his baseline, begins tapping or drumming his fingers on himself or on the table or something in front of him.

This is a very definite guilty indication as is the same fingers grooming his clothing. Perhaps seeing if that collar button is really buttoned or seeing if the cuff button is really buttoned or rolling up the sleeves or tucking in the shirt or any other sudden sign of grooming that is attempting to interrupt the flow of the conversation, relieve the stress, give the person time to subconsciously gather his thoughts. This also indicates heavy stress and probably lying.

The hands themselves also indicate heavy stress and often lying by the technique known as the "throw away". During this technique, a peak of tension question is asked and the interviewee will flip his hand away as though he was tossing something into a wastepaper basket. This flip when it's done to the side or in the front or from the chin indicates stress and lying. It indicates getting rid of this bothersome question, changing the subject, getting away from this area.

Another hand symbol which indicates the same lying, the same stress, is the white knuckle syndrome. This is the fight-or flight again. You can actually see someone's hands tense up and grip the chair or their knee or the table in front of them so tightly their knuckles lose blood and turn white. This is an almost definite indication of lying.

LEGS

Any swinging of the legs indicates stress or encountering a stressful situation. As the stress increases, as the interviewer narrows down the guilt-stress area, the swinging tends to increase both in force and speed. This is a direct indication of following the correct path.

The same thing is true with toe tapping. Toes may tap but if not established during the baseline period, it will indicate stress. If the tapping increases, both in length of taps so to speak (i.e., the entire foot may come off the floor), or in speed of tapping. This indicates a definite increase in stress, which a good kinesic interviewer will pick up on immediately.

The most stressful indication of footwork is when the interviewee poises his feet as though he were in a starting position for a race. In other words, one foot forward, one foot back, knees flexed as though he's about to run. Obviously, this dates back to the fight-or-flight syndrome and indicates exactly that. He wants to run. This is a heavy indication of deceitful behavior. Or lies.

If the legs and feet come out from under the chair and appear to relax, even now become more parallel in stance, this indicates the interviewee is more relaxed and the interviewer is less likely to receive the information he wants at this time. A good interviewer will press back into a stressful situation or employ one of the other techniques we've already discussed to induce stress. He will watch for the legs to return under the chair to indicate he's on the right track and is on the verge of getting a confession or at least on the verge of finding out something he wants to find out.

Use this wisely. Watch your feet as well as the other symbols and signs of your body in order to mislead the interviewer either in the wrong direction or simply negate any evidence of stress or guilt.

CENTRAL BODY ATTACKING

Once the interviewer feels he has control of the situation due to the various things we've all ready discussed, or even before in some cases, he may imply an interesting technique known as "attacking the central body zones".

This technique although deceptively simple does work. In order to do this the interviewer as he is talking to you normally during the tension type questions, will begin gesturing at the sensual part of your body, usually your chest or your stomach. These gestures will not be threatening in themselves. That is they're not punches or slaps, but rather points, direct points, sudden points, or other normal gestures that would happen during a conversation of this type.

All of these gestures are pointed toward your central, middle body zone. Coupled with the leaning forward violation of your vulnerability circle, these attitudes, these actions will often create a reaction in the interviewee that he is being attacked even though he's not physically being attacked. This will produce a feeling of insecurity in the abdominal-stomach area of the person.

In all martial arts, oddly enough, and in many Chinese schools of thought and Chinese schools of medicine, a person's soul or a person's Tai or Chi resides in his stomach or in the area directly under it. This is from where a Sumo wrestler or a karate master gathers his strength. It is this area that is being made to feel impotent and insecure by these hand movements. If successful the feeling in the interviewee is often one of helplessness, hopelessness or even one of wanting to regain the strength by copping out to the interviewer. Be aware of these techniques. Do not be brought closer to the point of admission or feel like you are in a weakened position because of these movements.

Yes, this is easier to say than it is to do. The trick is to practice. Have a friend who has a vicious streak in him, sit down and go over our photos and this portion of the book and attempt to do this with you until you can read the symbols during a normal conversation and until you become non-advantage to your enemy. It is a cut--your enemy has a sword and it's cutting your stomach area. You're not going to let this happen by drawing on your stomach's strength.

One system of doing this, if you can do this without being obvious, is to take fairly deep breaths. To concentrate on a point about 2 inches below your navel. This is the point in which martial artists believe your strength or your Tai is stored. If you can take a number of deep breaths while concentrating on this area, maintaining a relaxed look on your face, and not being threatened by these gestures, the speed of the gestures or the closeness of the interviewer, you will find the strength emanating from you which may actually reverse the tables and make the interviewer uncomfortable rather than the interviewee.

Also understand by applying these tactics the interviewer is admitting he is in a position where he needs to apply great pressure and is trying to trip you into a sudden confession or sudden slip. This should mean to you that you are in a position of strength and he is in a position of weakness and trying to force the situation by a potentially dangerous, psychologically dangerous attitude.

Practice accepting the attitude of "no attitude". In other words, there's no need for hiding. There's no need for feeling threatened. You are open on all sides. You have nothing to hide. Your stomach is strong. Your Tai is strong. Your Chi is strong. No simple hand gesture, hand movement or leaning forward on anyone's part is threatening to you at all. On the other hand, it may appear to seem odd to you that this person would do this. The interviewer will often pick this up and will feel odd doing it. He'll have lost a crucial point in the interview.

Remember the entire kinesic interview or any other type of truth-lie, flight or stand interview is an exercise in strategy. In strategy there is a way, a way that works. In strategy your spiritual bearing must be no different from your normal bearing. Any deviation will be picked up by a successful interviewer or by a smart machine. Your spirit should be settled, yet unbiased. You should be calm, yet not totally relaxed.

Remember an elevated spirit is weak and a very low spirit is weak. Do not let your interviewer read your spirit. This is the basis of successful kinesic interviewing.

PERSONALITY ASSESSMENT THROUGH EYE MOVEMENTS

An extremely important part of kinesic interviewing is to be able to ascertain the general type of personality of the interviewee.

There's a quick and easy way to do this and it's almost foolproof. That is to watch the person's eyes during the baseline control portion of the interview, and occasionally during the peak of tension portion to see which way they look. Most people will look either to the left or to the right subconsciously ever so often during a conversation. It's almost as though they are looking for something they expect to be there or they are doing it while they are thinking. It's sort of the old comic strip, "Hmmmm" with a balloon over the head and the eyes go to one side. This is a very natural reaction and if you can watch yourself on video tape you'll find you do it.

How does this help a kinesic interviewer? Simple. A person who is normally introverted would usually shift his gaze on a regular basis during the interview to the left when he breaks eye contact. On the other hand an extroverted person will look to the right when he breaks eye contact.

Watch this. If the pattern is soon established, it becomes a very useful factor for the interviewer. How so? Simple. If they are dealing with an introverted personality, the experienced kinesic interviewer will force the person into a stressful situation as soon as possible. He will give the person little room to run. He will force him into a fight-or-flight syndrome immediately because introverted people are much more subject to stress and will confess much more readily when placed in stressful situations.

A good kinesic interviewer may use many more structured questions, not lying of course, but slipping around the truth during this stage with the expectation of getting a confession from the introverted person.

If the person appears to be an extroverted personality, the kinesic strategy is quite different. The person must be treated with respect. He must be shown logical and rational reasons to confess, to give up his guilt. This can often take the form of siding with the person, downplaying the severity of the situation, etc., but it must be a logical approach. Sometimes he will even play to the person's ego, "Boy, the person who pulled that off was really a genius."

If introverted they must be browbeaten into a confession. Extroverted people must be respected and shown reasons why they should confess or show signs of guilt.

KINESIC INTERVIEWING; ADVANCED TECHNIQUES

Kinesic interviewing is a relatively young science and as such is still progressing. There have been some further developments or further refinements in techniques even since we have written the first section of this book. Therefore, we want to include a few refinements in the technique or additional information or clarification of information. Nothing contradicts what we have already taught and nothing will replace what we have already taught.

Let's begin with some vocal techniques.

VOCAL TECHNIQUES

Flight phrases are a good signpost of someone who is not telling the truth. In other words, people who demand to be taken as truthful, people who vocalize, "I'm telling you the truth; listen, I'm not lying at all," generally are overdoing it to the sense of trying to hide the fact that they are indeed lying.

Another way this is often phrased is someone will say, "Well, you know, you're just trying to tell the truth and then people will think you're lying." Anyone who has to advise that people will think he's lying, especially when he's not been accused of lying at this point (in other words, he himself, the subject, has brought up the phrase, "people think I'm lying," or "everyone thinks you're lying," or "there's no use doing this because they just think you're lying"), is generally lying. If he was telling the truth there was really no reason to bring up the question of lying at this point. This is a fairly standard and fairly reliable indicator of a falsehood.

Any noticeable change in pitch during the questioning procedure, especially during sensitive or relative questions (normally this means a rising pitch), is an indicator of stress and lying. This is often seen better in men than wormen, especially men who talk with a relatively low voice, whose voice suddenly seems to break or crack and the pitch rises.

Giggling or laughing can also be an indication of falsehoods. However, this must be used in conjunction with an established base line. The examiner will have talked to the person and asked non-stressful or nonrelevant questions enough to have realized if the person giggles, laughs or uses other such covering signs during a normal conversation. If during the base line portion of the test they do not, additions of this nature are held to be an indicator of falsehood.

A good interviewer will re-ask or rearrange these stressful questions and reintroduce them to see if the same reaction prevails or if other signs of falsehood are present at this time. If the subject does start giggling or laughing, it is often useful to keep the stressful questions coming in a non-stop manner in order to force the issue. But bear in mind one always has to have a base line to go on when looking for any form of stressful reactions. Some people may giggle or laugh or change pitch or use their hands in normal questioning or normal conversation. Some people are more nervous than others. It's the interviewer's job to both make the person not nervous enough to exhibit stress except under falsehood situations and to establish, note and maintain his base line.

BODY PROTECTION MOVEMENTS

A common form of body protection is scratching the back of the head or the neck. This may look normal when viewed alone but in context with other stressful indicators, it can be taken as a symbolic gesture of protecting one's neck. If you think back to any sort of threat or death movements, the cutting of the neck with the finger is a common way to indicate trouble. By lifting the hand up to the neck, it is symbolically protecting the neck. Once it's there, you have to do something with it. The normal reaction is scratching. Additional indicators of body protection are: adjusting the tie, fixing the cuffs, flicking pieces of lint off the clothes, etc., and anything that will raise the hands to the neck or central core of the body in a protective type movement.

A stuttering or stuttering type sound, if it is not done in the base line (for instance, if they say, "No, no, no, no" rapidly, in sequence) is a good indicator of stress.

It's important to remember one single indicator alone does not indicate lying. It may indicate nervousness or stress. After the base line is established, a good interviewer looks for clusters - that is, giggling, laughing, stuttering, coupled with neck protection, or turning away. Any cluster of stressful movements is very likely to indicate a falsehood. Beginning interviewers often get carried away and see someone scratch his head and think, "obviously he's telling a lie." Well, he could have had an itch in his head. These things do happen and one cannot be over sympathetic or over sensitive to the subject. That's why it's so important to establish the base line is so important to establish correctly and then watch for clusters during the stressful part of the questioning.

Clusters can be defined verbally as at least two stressful indications - that is giggling, then stuttering "No, no, no, no" or stuttering and then saying, "This is the truth, this is the truth. I wouldn't lie." Those two different indicators will normally indicate a stressful situation and probably a falsehood. Physically, scientists believe it takes four different movements out of the ordinary, above the base line, to indicate a falsehood in the stressful part of the questioning. Anything less than this cannot be judged a cluster.

It's at this stage that most subjects who have any training or knowledge of kinesic interviewing, will overdo the control portion of these movements. That is, their movements will become very pointed and they will think each one through before doing it, they will appear to be holding themselves back from normal movements or normal body shifting. This, to a very observant kinesic interviewer, will point out stress also. The way to approach a kinesic interview situation is to <u>convince yourself you are innocent and act as though you are innocent. Do not attempt to think through each movement, simply relax, let your base line be established as you wish in normal conversation and then focus your mind elsewhere, if necessary, as shown in the polygraph interview techniques. Simply act natural and normal. Do not worry about each little movement or take back a movement once it has started. Relax and appear normal.</u>

The best way to do this is rationalize the situation to yourself to where you really believe you're not lying. If there are reasons for doing what you did, if you think everyone else does it, whatever type of rationalization it takes, once you've rationalized to yourself that you are not lying, you will, in fact, be much more likely to appear truthful to any kinesic interviewer. It is also possible to deliberately exaggerate the base line portion of the test, if you know that's what is happening, by adding movements which you have videotaped or observed yourself doing when you're in a stressful situation in normal conversation. In other words, exaggerating your hand movements, laughing if that's what you tend to do, shifting your eyes - if you establish a high base line and that is thought to be your normal way of speech, chances are these things will be discounted or not counted as clusters during the stressful portion of the kinesic interview.

If you think you are going to be subjected to kinesic interviewing, note the base line portion of the test. The interviewer will try and establish a norm by asking non-stressful questions, "How long have you been working here? How do you like it? What's your job exactly? What did you do before this? Do you enjoy this part of the country?" He's simply trying to get you to talk, answer questions that are not stressful and observe your reactions in order to form a mental picture of your movements for comparison to the stressful portion of the test.

Another interesting giveaway to a kinesic interview situation is the interviewer will normally sit himself directly in front of the subject without any obstructions such as a desk or table between the two. The reason for this is for him to be able to observe the subject's entire body's reactions and not give the subject something he can touch or use to cover portions of his body or block stressful cluster signs.

A way to test this, for instance, is if he's sitting behind a desk and there's a chair next to the desk, he indicates you should sit there as the subject, pull the chair out directly in front of the interviewer so the desk is between the both of you and sit down. A good kinesic interviewer will not allow this to happen. He will either move you back or move himself around eliminating the obstacle between the two of you. This is a dead giveaway in a kinesic interview situation. Rarely will there ever be arms on the chairs or any other objects in the room to distract or to be able to be used as distractions by the subject.

STARING DOWN

If the subject attempts to stare down, that is maintain heavy eye contact to the point of aggressiveness with the interviewer, this is a good sign he is trying to take control of the interview and trying to make the interviewer feel nervous or out of place and can be taken as a stressful indicator or included at least in a cluster of physical indicators. It is not a good sign. Try to avoid doing it if you are a subject. It generally means the subject has something to hide and needs to control the situation to avoid giving it away.

Normal eye contact during a conversation is held to be 60% of the time. In other words, a person will move his eyes 40% of the time by blinking or concentrating on something else. Anything more than 60% eye contact is considered staring or staring down the opponent. This is also a cultural thing and actually 40 to 60% is considered normal for all cultures. Sixty percent is considered normal for Americans. Now remember breaking eye contact (during the 40% of the time you're not looking someone in the eyes) should be normal. People during a normal conversation will glance at the person's mouth, glance at the person's ears, blink, glance at their forehead. This is all well and good. However, avoid the direct breaks we mentioned earlier, such as looking at your fingernails, picking your fingernails, staring at the floor or other obvious indicators of stress.

Closing the eyes completely is often taken as a stressful sign unless you have established it during the base line that you do shut your eyes occasionally, rub them, or shut them during questioning. Occasionally people will do this, but if you don't do it during the norm part of the test and do it during the stress part, it's going to be taken as a stressful sign.

Emotionally or mentally disturbed people will maintain different eye contact levels. However, this will come out during the norm part of the test. Also, a good interviewer will try and establish your blink rate during the nonstressful questioning. An increase in blinking during the stressful questioning is taken as a definite indicator of stress.

We've already mentioned the carotid artery throbbing as a definite indicator of stress. It's also very possible for people, especially women although it does happen in men, to have their skin become blotchy or mottled as the arteries dilate and constrict with a stressful situation, changing the blood flow to the face. One way to avoid this, if you are a woman, is to use makeup, especially on your neck and face so the artery and the skin signs are not noticeable.

Remember the fight or flight syndrome. This is what the interviewer is looking for. Any aggressive movements such as staring down, leaning over the desk, that is trying to take over territory or shifting away and using any of the avoidance techniques we've mentioned, point out to the interviewer that he is approaching the right area and is getting stressful signs. A good interviewer will then close in on these questions, asking more direct questions, asking the crucial questions at this point because he knows you are becoming stressful. At this point he is very likely to force a confession or force a complete avoidance of the question, or at least force some definite action.

This can be done by several methods we've pointed out such as attacking the center of the body, etc. These are the indicators he will look for. If you find the interviewer narrowing in on the central area at issue, look at yourself closely and see if you are giving stressful indicators. If so, try to return to the norm without being obvious.

During the base line portion of the questioning, a kinesic interviewer will try to establish if the subject is an introverted or an extroverted type of person. The common method of doing this is by gauging the speed of his answers and their reaction time. An introverted person may be slow to answer, slightly shy, and hesitant. An extroverted person will often jump ahead and answer the question even before the interviewer has even stopped the question itself. He will break in the middle of sentences, being very quick to answer. If the interviewer is faced with an introvert, it is wrong to approach the stressful area too rapidly. In other words, you don't ask, "Did you murder so and so?" As you get to the stressful part of the questions, you say, "Did you hurt or did you accidentally hurt so and so?"

The abrupt jump to heavy stress will cause an introvert to completely shut down, negating the rest of the questioning. If the person seems to be an extrovert, you can go right into the stressful or crucial points at hand because they are going to deal with it in the manner in which you want them to deal with it.

PICTURE PAINTING

Once the interviewer has detected signs of stress and feels he has narrowed the questioning to the crucial areas with the correct responses, he may paint a picture. This is a verbal montage where he will recreate the scene of the crime in a hypothetical sense. "Now just suppose you did go into the room on your lunch break, and suppose it was empty. Marsha was not at her desk and suppose the money was on the desk unattended."

Now during this stage, the interviewer is not waiting for the answer to the question as much as he is watching the reaction of the subject. A classical guilt and about-to-confess reaction is for the subject to look up at the beginning of the picture painting, maybe even above the interviewer's eyes at the ceiling, and then his eyes will gradually drop down and roll to the floor, as the crucial part of the question gets closer. This indicates guilt. In some situations, a guilt-ridden subject will actually drop his head onto his chest, rolling his eyes all the way to the floor. This indicates he is about to confess. He's rehashing the crime in his head. He knows you know how it happened and he's about to confess to it.

By this time the interviewer has gathered enough information from the rest of the interview to paint a correct picture of what did happen. At this point, the interviewer may hit the subject with an escape route or a double edged questions. "You didn't really mean to hurt them, did you? It was an accident." or "You really didn't mean to take the money. You probably were planning on reporting it to the supervisor." You are giving them an out, a chance to save face. This will often induce a confession on the spot.

This is like asking, "When did you stop beating your wife?" There's really no way out of it. Try to avoid getting in these situations and if you do, simply deny it straightforwardly by saying, "Well, I didn't do it so I have no idea if that's what I would have done. It never entered my head. Sorry."

Do not over react. Do not go on. Do not deny it more than one time. Do not cut him off before the question is answered and deny it. Let him have his fun. Do not roll your eyes but keep normal eye contact, a normal pitch of voice and flat out deny the charges.

MASKING TENSION

The interviewer will watch for tension masking techniques through the entire interview, again comparing them to the base line. Anything that amounts to fidgeting, looking away, fixing your clothes, winding your watch, cleaning your glasses, picking lint, a good pipe smoker can waste five minute fidgeting with his pipe to make it look like useful movements, these are tension masks, trying to buy time, trying to get away. A good kinesic interviewer knows he's closing in on the crucial part of the subject and will not allow this to happen. He will increase the heaviness of the questions at this time.

If possible, practice tension relieving techniques at home with biofeedback, self-hypnosis, concentrating on something other than the question at hand, whatever works for you, before getting in this situation. When you are in a kinesic interview situation, watch for signs of tension in your back, the back of your arms, your hands, your knuckles. If you see them or if you can feel them, a good interviewer will, too. Try to avoid this and force yourself to relax and smile.

THE NOSE

If the interviewer is talking and the subject begins touching or playing with his nose, it's a good indicator he does not like what the interviewer is saying. If the subject is talking and begins touching or playing with his own nose, it's an almost definite indicator of a falsehood. Avoid the nose. Avoid anything that breaks the continuity of speech or interrupts the flow with a physical motion. This must be done without seeming to be too stiff or without obvious control.

This can be used to your advantage, too. When the interviewer is speaking and accusing the subject of doing something and the subject plays with his nose, he is saying, "No, I don't like what you're saying. You're wrong. I didn't do it." It's not a sign of innocence, but a sign of disagreement with the interviewer. Another time to use this disagreement nose technique is when the interviewer drops into his painting the picture stage and begins describing the scene. Start rubbing your nose. You disagree with him. That's not how it happened. You wouldn't have done that.

Head touching, if not done during the normal part of the test, is an indication of being right on the mark or inducing heavy stress. Be careful of this.

THE MOUTH

A false smile, gulping, licking the lips, cotton mouth, asking for a glass of water, these are all definite indicators of stress and/or falsehoods and should be avoided. This goes along with relaxing the body and appearing normal at all times.

If a person's face suddenly goes white and/or he clutches at it, it indicates a drop in blood pressure and the systems are shutting down. This is not a fight or flight syndrome. This is a simple shut down of systems, because it's an extremely stressful question or unexpected stress. It usually indicates the interviewer is right on the mark.

ISSUE AND STRESS

Remember there are two different types of questions that can bring on indications - issue questions and stress questions. Examples of issue questions are: what happened, how did it happen, describe it to me. The stress questions are: did you do it, are you guilty, were you in the store, are you familiar with the store, did you know the money was taken? These are all issue questions. The stress question following these would be, "Did you take it?"

During the issue questions if someone is getting the fight or flight syndrome, the blood pressure will go up, his skin will often get redder, he is internally debating whether to fight or flight the situation. Then you hit him with the crucial part of the question, the stress question, and he can go into shock. This indicates guilt. There is simply no way around it. Of course, there are other reactions, too, which indicate guilt as we've already seen.

OTHER BODY GIVEAWAYS

Some people as they begin to get stressful will begin to curve their body and will continue this until their head, neck and body almost entirely curves into a semicircle shape.

Do not slump unless you normally do. Do not go to sleep in the hall or the area prior to the test. This may sound ridiculous, but it is a fairly common reaction where someone who is extremely nervous will sleep. Any kinesic interviewer is going to be extremely wary of someone who can snooze off quickly, as that is the safest, fastest, easiest way to avoid the situation and avoid the problem.

Sometimes kinesic interviewers will seat their subjects in front of a tile wall or a wall with lines and when you view a tape showing this, it is possible to see the subject bending off center from the line gradually as the stress increases until he's almost 45 degrees off center. To a kinesic interviewer this is known as a stress meter or degree of line.

CHIN

If a person is holding his chin in his dominant hand and smiling slightly, it is taken as a sign he is about to confess. In other words, you've caught on. The game is up. If he has his hand on his chin with his finger up the side of his face and not really supporting the chin, it is a sign of antagonism or arrogance. The latter tells the interviewer you are fighting and there is some stress there, and he's probably in the right area even though you're not ready to confess.

If the head position is slightly tilted, it means the person is interested and probably following what you are saying. If the head is tilted forward and the chin is touching the sternum, he's given up and it's now time to force a confession. Do not do this.

HANDS AND ARMS

Any unusual activity with the hands, such as rubbing the legs, which is a self-assurance gesture, fidgeting, preening, messing with your hair, hiding your hands under your legs or behind your back, fluttering them, moving them, are signs of deception as are marked non-movements. These include stiffness, holding in, etc. This may sound like a no win situation - you can't move your hands - you can't keep them still. The idea is to be aware of your normal activity which you have established during the base line period of the test, and stick to it. Any deviation in either direction will cause stressful thinking on the part of the interviewer.

Keep your hands out of your face and your hair, but if you normally use gestures when talking, use those gestures. Crossing of the arms, especially in women, indicates a defensive posture, and protection of the breasts or central area; "fig-liking," especially by men, (in a standing position, putting their hands over their crotch), all indicate definite stress.

SUMMARY - TRUTH OR DECEPTION INDICATORS

TRUTH

To indicate truth you appear to be at ease, you do not exhibit tense shoulders, back, neck or arms, you're talkative, you appear to be answering questions directly but not chatty or cutting off the questioner. You're at ease and not avoiding the subject. You are not diffusing the issue, you're answering the question. Good eye contact and light hearted conversation, because it's no big deal, you didn't do it, you're not guilty.

But not to the extremes of silly, light heartedness, not direct attempts to change the conversation into, "Oh, what a lovely office. Is that a picture of your wife and kids?" Avoid out of context conversation and being a subject changer.

LYING

The subject is going to be apprehensive. He's worried, he may sigh or yawn, which releases stress, in fact, a real live yawn not a fake yawn, relieves a ton of stress. The interviewer will be on the watch for this. A fake yawn is a hiding syndrome, giving yourself a chance to think, which is just as bad, but too many yawns is a definite indicator of stress. Beware of this. It also tends to give you more oxygen than you have had, perking you up and giving you a chance to think. This is also an indicator of tenseness as you need more oxygen when your muscles are tense.

Aggressiveness or being overly friendly, poor eye contact or the opposite, attempting to stare down the interviewer, evasive answers, excessive movement or absence of movement, all that differs from the norm established during the base line portion of the test. These all indicate undue stress.

Muscle movement indicates stress as it tends to relieve tension. Often this begins in the legs as the legs are some of the largest muscles in the body and, therefore, can relieve stress quickly. Shifting position, shifting the buttocks, crossing or uncrossing the legs, are all indications of emotion and if observed during the stressful portion of the test, indicate stress and/or guilt.

PROXIMITY

A normal kinesic interviewer will begin the questions at a comfortable distance from the subject. If a subject begins showing signs of stress, he may move in gradually, in a non-threatening manner. In fact, he may move in so far as to prevent the subject from crossing or uncrossing his legs by putting one of his knees between the subject's legs. This is done to help keep the level of stress he has noticed high, make the subject more uncomfortable, make him exhibit stress in other directions since he can no longer relieve it in this direction, and force him into a fight or flight syndrome. This is the point where the subject will usually blow it.

Now as the subject, if you notice the interviewer is moving in and closing the proximity, is attempting to stop your stress relieving motions, you've started to blow it already. An honest person should not get to this stage. This is stage three. Stage one being the base line and stage two being the stress indicators while stage three being the point where he has determined you are probably guilty and is trying to force you into a compromising position and hopefully a confession.

If you have let the situation get to this position, the best move to do at this point, is put both hands behind your neck, spread your arms, lean backwards in an opening position as shown in one of my photos, and just simply relax. This is the position of non-attack or open on all sides, the position from which it is impossible to force a stressful reaction or confession from anyone. The interviewer will try to block this position and go back over the questions that caused you stress in an attempt to close your body up or will attack your middle zone in an attempt to get you to be defensive. Do not. Maintain this position, maintain your relaxed, neutral answers, don't fidget, and eventually he will be forced into giving up, taking you as an uncooperative subject or that he made a mistake the first time and you are actually not lying, just stressful because of being interviewed. This is known as the uninterrogation position.

If you are not an acquaintance or a friend, the distance of six to 18 inches from the subject is known as personal space and will keep one under stress simply by the interviewer's proximity. The interviewer, as he detects stress, may move into this distance simply to keep up this stress. Obviously if you back away or attempt to move or hide the stressful gestures, he will continue along this path of questioning and movements to attempt to induce a confession from you.

A sure sign of the interviewer suspecting you is when he begins to move in from his normal interviewing distance of five or six feet and gradually close the distance to this personal distance that you would normally allow no one but a close friend into. Try not to be defensive. Go into the open on all eight sides position, relax, don't be nervous.

Proximity is a three step process. One usually begins at the normal interviewing distance, establish a base line of the subject's movement and reactions, and then move on to the issue questions from the same distance to see his reactions and if stress is present. If he shows definite indications of stress, a change from the base line, then the interviewer will proceed to step three and intrude upon his space forcing the stress even higher and concentrate on the stressful areas as shown by the step two questioning. This third step is designed to stop the subject from being able to relieve stress - crossing his legs, stretching, scratching, yawning, etc. It is difficult but if you've come to this stage, you are already losing. It's time to relax or go to our uninterrogation position.

At certain times a good interviewer will force the issue to the point, i.e., if he moves in when your legs are already crossed, you cannot uncross them and can be getting very uncomfortable, the subject will have to ask the interviewer to please move so he can uncross his legs. This is an ideal position as the subject now owes the interviewer one and is on the defensive.

CONFESSION RED FLAGS

Palms turned upward, sighing, drooping shoulders, head down, chin down to the throat, look at the ceiling and look back slowly, crying, blinking your eyes slowly, opening the body completely, relax, slump, he's given up. At this point a good kinesic interviewer expects and usually will get, a confession. Also, holding the chin with the dominant hand and a slight smile or placing your head down into the other person's face as in a Japanese bow meaning, "I give up. You win." These are all confession indicators.

Body signals of confession include leaning forward into the other person's space, rubbing one's lips together for an extended period of time, say 15 to 30 seconds, like you are getting ready to talk, and an overall look of submission. When the interviewer sees any of these signals , he must soon afterwards lower his voice and ask the crucial question and then shut up. This silence is the last guilt indicator needed to make the person want to fill the space and he's going to fill it with a confession. If the interviewer keeps talking, he can talk someone right out of a confession.

CONCLUSIONS

The use of the Kinesic Interview Technique is dependent upon inducing stress and guilt and a wanting to confess in the interviewee. A good interviewer will go over this technique until it becomes secondhand, second nature to use the techniques we've discussed.

By the same token, a good interviewee, that is one who wants to pass a kinesic interview, will do the same thing. This is up to you. You must re-read this book as well as to utilize the practice methods we've discussed. If you have access to a video tape unit, use it. If you have access to a tape recorder, use that. If you have access to any friends, use them. What the hell. If not, find a relative.

The point is to go over each section and learn to lead the interview in the direction you want it to go rather than be controlled by the interviewer.

Again, this is likened to a fight situation in which you are not to be on the defensive the entire time, but rather to lead your attacker where you want him to go, even if you don't attack back. By direct communication you are attacking back.

By using your spirit and either parrying the enemy's attack or by using your spirit to calm the flow and to maintain the kinesic attitude necessary, you'll led the interview where you want it to go. Your attitude, your non-attitude, your timing, your eye contact, your gaze, your stance, your verbal and nonverbal responses, even recognizing the formulated portions of the interview peak of tension questions, will help greatly. It will allow you to polish your strategy in order to "pass" any kinesic interview.

These same principles can be applied to non-kinesic interviews. Since some of this is obviously gut-level material, you'll find these ideas apply to almost any interview situation. They can even apply to calming someone down when he is angry or to find out something you want to know.

Also read the rest of this book, please, and understand there are possible applications of artificial methods to also influence the outcome of a kinesic interview.

Even learning the polygraph test method and how it works, will give you some idea of how the Kinesic Interview Technique works also. They are all intertwined, they all go together.

You must master this way of strategy in order to beat the machine or beat the interviewer. You must become a rock. You must become normal. You must become unvarying, and you must become confident. The way to do this is practice, practice, practice.

An example of a state of the art five function polygraph. This model available from Lafayette Instrument Co, Inc.

the most popular five-pen polygraphs

These two models represent the two top selling of Lafayette's five-pen instruments. Their appeal is understandable since they contain the capability to record all of the parameters an examiner could ever want, including mechanical cardio, mechanical pneumo, electro-cardio, electro-pneumo, and with a full 6-inch curvelinear pen swing. With the purchase of two of Lafayette's accessories, heart rate and peripheral vasomotor activity (ple) can be recorded as well. With this instrument the examiner has his/her choice of running simultaneous pneumo and/or simultaneous cardio along with GSR. For the purpose of recording dual cardio, a second sphygmomanometer is available.

DIPLOMAT SAMSONITE ATTACHE

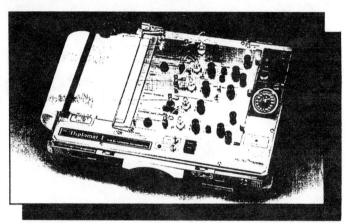

Model **761-99GA**   **$3,975.00**

Other important features of these models are; inclusion of an all-purpose amplifier with capabilities to record electro-cardio, electro-pneumo, and auxiliary function, plus that all-important GSR. With the all-purpose amplifier you never need worry about a GSR malfunction. Should that occur you need only replace the standard recording pen with the pen from your GSR module, switch the mode selector to GSR and you are ready to resume testing. It's that easy. Of course, either multi-function or all-purpose amplifier can now be purchased with the latest development in cardio recording, auto response. Addition of auto response eliminates manual adjustment of a response control to arrive at an acceptable recording. If you are one of those examiners who would like to eliminate that extra step in pretest preparation.

AMBASSADOR HALLIBURTON ALUMINUM

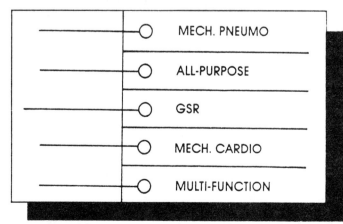

Model **761-95GA**   **$3,875.00**

POLYGRAPH USE AND COUNTERMEASURES

POLYGRAPH RESEARCH AND SUBSEQUENT ANALYSIS

There have been volumes and volumes of works, papers and studies funded by universities, associations and the government to prove or disprove the validity of the polygraph. Most of these papers involve situations where mock crimes are set up and students usually paid a small fee for their participation or other subjects are set up to act out the part of the guilty or the innocent person in this mock crime situation.

There are several things to realize right in the beginning about this type of testing. In the first place we're not going to pad this book by loading it down with these tests. Anyone who is interested can find much, much material on these tests and, in fact, people from both sides of the polygraph fence can point to statistics which will verify their own position. Some studies have shown very heavy, that is 90 - 100% correct identification of guilty parties, although the innocent generally runs a little less than that. Other studies will show the same 50% as pure chance or as less than chance.

Some of the key phrases to watch for in these tests are: significantly better than chance (that's a great sounding phrase, but would you want your neck to hang on it?). You'll notice it doesn't say 100% or positively. It says significantly better than chance. Somehow this does not elicit a great amount of emotional stability in me. Perhaps it's just my flawed judgment, but I'd rather not be subjected to a test that may be "greater than chance".

Also many of these tests have another catchy phrase called: admitting inconclusives, whereby any inconclusive or any report or chart that is judged inconclusive by the operator is tossed out. This, of course, brings the percentage of correct answers up significantly as the tests which may have gone either way or which you would have to classify as innocent because there really wasn't enough data to classify as guilty, are thrown out. This is called "weighting the test" and is done in most studies. This invalidates many, many studies right in the beginning of the study.

Typically we can take some studies, i.e., those done by Horvath in '77 which are recognized as some of the best in the field where good examiners were used, the control question procedures were standard and correct, at least three pen recorders were used, all examinations included two charts, plus the stimulation test, there were a high number of examinations, etc. - in other words, a fairly random sampling of good lie detection testing techniques.

In this particular test that I'm quoting the original examiner decision was based on all the information in the polygraph examination. Then ten other examiners were allowed to see the charts alone. In other words, they had not been there during the tests, and made their evaluations from the charts alone. Now this presents an interesting quandary. For verified cases in this particular test, 51% of the truthful cases were classified as truthful by the examiner and 77% of the deceptive cases were classified as deceptive by the actual examiner. Even this is not very good when you stop and look at it. Fifty-one percent of the truthful cases were classified as truthful, one percent more than chance? He did slightly better on the deceptive cases, but still not conclusive by a long shot.

When the charts were examined by the independent examiners this ratio of correct to incorrect decisions dropped significantly indicating that the examiner used other techniques, perhaps gut-level feelings or Kinesic Interview Techniques to bias his judgments during the test.

This would have to be considered a typical test. Again this is a laboratory situation and laboratory situations and mock crimes differ greatly from actual crimes or actual situations in which the subject has something to lose - possibly his life.

There are other problems with these studies. First, they do not provide information about the validity of the original examiner's decisions unless the original examiner makes his decision using only information from the polygraph charts (this is more likely when numerical scoring is used). In most cases the original examiner uses both the polygraph charts and additional information in his decision (e.g., subject behavior and case information). Since the two decisions were based on different types of information, these studies will only provide information on the validity of the blind evaluator's decision based solely on the polygraph charts.

It is debatable whether these studies are even validity studies of the blind evaluator's decision because the description of sample selection in most of the studies suggests only verified cases confirming the original examiner's decision were used. If cases where the original examiner's decision is incorrect are eliminated from the sample, the sample has a very restricted range. A true validity study also would investigate how the blind examiner scores the cases not correctly classified by the original examiner. However, incorrect decisions were not necessarily eliminated. All of the verified cases Horvath found in 1977 agreed with the original examiner's decision. Thus, there is enough confusion in the reporting of sample selection in all of the studies using verified cases to make them problematical.

It could be said that use of a restricted sample of only those verified cases confirming the original examiner's decision would overestimate the validity of the blind examiner's decision and that validity could not be any higher than what is reported in these studies. However, it is possible that the type of decision the original examiner makes influences the polygraph test. For example, the original examiner making a clinical judgment from subject behavior, case facts and polygraph charts may make a decision sooner, possibly with fewer charts, than an examiner who uses only numerical scoring. If the type of decision an examiner makes influences the examination procedure, these studies should not be considered as evidence for the validity of the blind examiner's decision.

Also lack of independence between examiner decision and the criterion can occur in several ways and it is impossible to determine the extent the non-independence influences the percentage of correct classifications. The examiner can influence the trial process either by increasing the probability of conviction or that charges are dropped. This is a particular problem in the Peters study involving subject guilt or innocence in only 11 cases, but it is unclear the extent to which the results of the polygraph test were influential in the decision to go to trial or drop charges. Confession also is not independent of the polygraph examination. Examiners usually interrogate only those showing physiological responses to relevant questions. Thus, those showing no deceptive responses will be under less pressure to confess. It also is possible to induce a false confession, although that is extremely rare. Some researchers think the use of confession invalidates the study, others think confession is acceptable as a criterion.

Another example of different ways of looking at the same situation was accomplished by a test given by the Army in which 250 questions were asked to a large sample of people. Surprisingly the over-all test scores appeared pretty good - 86% of the guilty and 76% of the innocent were correctly identified. They used three different methods to identify the guilty and innocent parties. All three methods were able to identify deceptive subjects significantly greater than chance, once the inconclusives were, of course, thrown out. However, only the zone comparison and relevant-irrelevant methods were able to identify the non-deceptive subjects at any greater than chance rate.

When you stop to look at the actual question-by-question scoring rather than the overall test scoring, it becomes quite different. In this one the relevant-irrelevant method was the only method of the three able to identify deceptive questions significantly greater than chance. This was just barely greater than chance ranging from 54 - 69%, again omitting inconclusives. Non-deceptive questions did better and were rated greater than chance by all three methods.

Still you can see the inconclusive data can be gathered and the way statistics can be weighted in almost all these studies.

Let's look at a closer analysis of some of the research that's been done. Bear in mind this analysis was written by someone very experienced in the field, although definitely on the side of the polygraph instrument itself. Still, if you read this analysis closely, you will discover many helpful things regarding the possibility of deception in the polygraph instrument itself and the rates of truthfulness and deception that these machines are able to do.

ANALYSIS OF RESEARCH

ANALYSIS

Several observations can be made about the research. First, the research literature is burgeoning. There has been more scientific research conducted on lie detection in the last six years than in the previous 60 years. Second, the polygraph technique is a robust technique. Although there are numerous variables which affect its accuracy, it works better than chance in a wide range of testing situations including criminal investigations, intelligence operations, security screening, mock crimes in a laboratory environment, and even games in which a person denies what number he selected. Indeed, it is difficult to find experiments in which lie detection did not work better than chance. The technique obviously works well with many cultures because many of the studies were conducted in Poland, Israel, and Japan. Third, there is no such thing as a perfect study. Each study is flawed; sometimes in its design, often in its execution, and sometimes in the selection, analysis, and reporting of the data. Occasionally the shortcomings are so serious as to disqualify the study from serious attention. Fortunately, the various studies usually contribute to the mosaic of our understanding of the polygraph technique and the factors which affect its accuracy. Our understanding of these variables has expanded rapidly within the last five to ten years with the accelerating pace of research.

Nonetheless, it is difficult to estimate the precise accuracy of the polygraph technique in everyday applications because of the number of variables involved. There are a variety of polygraph applications, each with its peculiar problems and issues: criminal investigation, intelligence operations, pre-employment screening and aperiodic security screening of current employees. Within each of these applications are many subcategories. Polygraph accuracy is probably different for each of these settings; however, some general comments about error rates can be made.

There is evidence to suggest that control question tests may be more accurate in detecting the deception of the guilty person than in verifying the truthfulness of the innocent person; that is, given equal numbers of guilty and innocent persons, more inconclusive results may occur with the innocent persons, and the number of false positives may outnumber the number of false negatives. Studies of this type have primarily found either more false positives than false negatives or essentially no difference in the false positives and false negative error rate. There are a few studies that found fewer false positives (Reid & Horvath, 1971; and Bersh 1969). Since the variables determine whether or not a study showed differential error rates have not been determined, it is unknown whether a preponderance of false positive errors is characteristic of field polygraph usage.

Additional evidence that the guilty may be easier to detect was reported by Barland & Raskin (1975). They found that the absolute values of scores from guilty subjects in a mock crime were more extreme than the scores from the innocent subjects, indicating that the size of the reactions of the guilty subjects on the relevant questions were larger than those of the innocent subjects on the control questions. They also found that on numerically scored control question tests of criminal suspects, the scores of the suspects called deceptive by the examiner were more extreme than the scores of the suspects called truthful by the examiner (Barland & Raskin, 1976). <u>Not all of those decisions could be verified, however.</u>

It is of interest to note that in two of the studies reporting a preponderance of false positives (Horvath, 1977; Kleinmuntz and Szucko, 1982) the errors occurred during the blind analysis of the polygraph charts. When verified cases were selected for study, no known errors were found regarding the polygraph tests as conducted by the original examiners. This suggests the possibility that the clinical judgment of the examiner who is able to observe the subject's demeanor throughout the test may serve as a

64

safeguard against false positive errors that may occur when the polygraph charts are interpreted in isolation from nonpolygraphic sources of data.

Peak of tension tests and especially the guilty knowledge test incorporate an extremely effective safeguard against false positive errors--the innocent person cannot determine which question is the critical question, and therefore cannot consistently react to it regardless of how nervous or fearful he is. Thus, with the peak of tension and guilty knowledge tests, virtually all errors are false negative errors. However, these tests can rarely be used in applications of the polygraph.

The base rates of truthfulness and deception within the specific population being examined can have effects on the proportion of false positive and false negative errors. The confidence to be placed in a given test outcome will vary according to the proportion of false positive and false negative results compared to the base rates of truthfulness and deception. As the base rate for deception decreases there is probably an increase in the number of false negative errors and a decrease in the number of false positive errors.

Another variable affecting the error rate is the type of issue to be resolved. The polygraph is believed to be most accurate when the subject denies having committed a specific physical act, such as a theft. Although there is, as yet, no research on this matter, several theories predict that the accuracy is reduced when the issue is vague or ambiguous, such as when the subject admits having shot the victim, but claims he had only intended to frighten, not kill, him. The polygraph issue is then one of intent, not the act. The extent to which the accuracy is reduced depends upon a number of factors unique to each case, such as the nature of the issue, the psychological makeup of the person being examined, the length in formulating and defining the precise test questions.

The polygraph is said to be most accurate when only one issue is to be resolved. When more than one issue must be included in the tests, as often happens in many intelligence applications and in pre-employment screening, the accuracy would, presumably, be less. However, in the absence of extensive research on this issue, it is not known whether the accuracy is reduced.

It is clear that the examiner's level of experience affects the accuracy of decisions. It may be that once a certain threshold has been reached additional experience results in only slight increases in accuracy, due to the inherent robustness of the technique. However, the critical level of experience has not been determined. Within the government, the closely supervised internship and the quality control review process assists the intern in conducting his examinations properly.

The approach to decision making (clinical versus numerical analysis of polygraph charts) undoubtedly affects the accuracy of the decisions, but this factor has not been adequately researched. It may be that the clinical approach may be important in safeguarding against false positive errors while the numerical evaluation approach minimizes false negative errors. If this proves to be true, than a combination of these approaches should minimize both types of error.

The number of polygraph charts obtained from a given subject may be related to the accuracy of the decisions. Generally, the more physiological information available to the examiner the more accurate his decisions are.

One of the complicating factors in trying to use the available research to estimate the accuracy of the polygraph in real life situations is the fact that many laboratory studies are conducted by researchers who have not been trained in the field uses of the polygraph. Among the many differences that lack of field training generates is the relative lack of interaction between the researcher and the subject. There are many things that can cause responses to appear to indicate deception on the polygraph charts. These include extraneous noises, visual distractions, emotional complexes associated with some word in a question, and even random thoughts. The accuracy of the polygraph technique depends largely upon the ability of the examiner to control the testing environment so that extraneous sources of reactions are eliminated. "Lie detection" can properly be thought of as an inference based upon a process of elimination. One important way in which the field examiner determines whether a subject may be reacting to a question for some reason other than deception is to talk to the subject between charts to find out what was going through his mind on various questions. The questions are then restructured based on the information the subject provides. This procedure would almost certainly reduce the number of innocent subjects classified as deceptive in laboratory tests.

In addition to polygraph accuracy, polygraph utility also is important. Utility refers to the ability of a test or procedure to produce the results desired. If 100 tests are administered, it is desired that 100 correct decisions be obtained. Anything which reduces the number of desired results reduces the utility of the test.

As applied to the polygraph, utility has several aspects. In one sense it refers to the ability of the polygraph examiner to obtain useful information from a subject as a result of the test regardless of the actual accuracy of the polygraph in terms of chart interpretation. During the interview conducted by the examiner immediately prior to attaching the subject to the polygraph, many subjects confess or reveal information they had not mentioned to previous investigators. The psychological "demand characteristics" of the polygraph situation are very powerful and should not be underestimated. Thus, even if the polygraph were not at all accurate, it would have a certain utility as long as people believed that it worked.

A second aspect of utility relates to the inconclusive rate. Even the most accurate test has diminishing utility as the inconclusive rate increases. Fingerprints, for example, have limited utility in investigations despite their extremely high accuracy because only occasionally can identifiable prints be recovered. In reference to the polygraph, it is necessary to distinguish between its utility and its accuracy. Utility in this respect refers to the total number of correct decisions out of the total number of cases; that is, the total number of cases minus both the inconclusive results and the errors. Accuracy, on the other hand, refers to the number of correct decisions out of the total number of decisions, after the inconclusive results have been set aside.

It is not possible to estimate the accuracy of the polygraph in Department of Defense work, at present, for the reasons discussed.

THE GSR: THE AFFORDABLE LIE DETECTOR

The GSR or Galvanic Skin Response Monitor is a device designed to measure minute electrical resistance changes in a subject's skin. The first polygraph was simply a GSR. Today some extremely inexpensive machines are simply more sophisticated versions of this first GSR. Almost without exception every polygraph unit uses the GSR as its main testing criteria.

The principle behind Galvanic Skin Response is that when a person lies or becomes unduly stressful, his involuntary nervous system causes his glands to secrete or sweat, if you will, more than when he is telling the truth. As sweat is essentially salty in nature, it is a very good conductor of electricity. Any minute sweating or gland excretions will cause the resistance of the skin to change noticeably.

The GSR employs an electronic bridge to measure these minute changes and translate them into an audible or visual measurement. The GSR is normally operated by attaching two electrodes to the subject's fingers. These electrodes may be held on with tape or, in the case of our unit, Velcro, to secure a tight electrical fit.

A professional quality GSR is invaluable in any experimentation having to do with polygraphs or lying as it will allow one to observe the body's involuntary nervous system's reactions, prove the ability of a lie detector to detect stress, and can also be employed as a practice device using various techniques we've covered and are going to cover here, to allow one to defeat or get around any type of polygraph device.

The unit we employed for our testing was a very satisfactory device and we recommend it for any of the exercises discussed for polygraph deception. In fact, it worked well enough that we would not hesitate to recommend its use as an inexpensive polygraph. Our GSR was provided by Bio Logic Devices, Inc., 81 Plymouth Road, Plainview, New York 11803. We used their Model 508. This retails in the neighborhood of $250 and employs a meter and a switchable audio indication in any change in galvanic skin response.

The first step is to become familiar with the unit itself, as you have three controls that vary sensitivity, volume and the null point as well as a function switch, power switch, and a polarity switch. This familiarization process will only take a few minutes as the device is fairly easy to use and the instructions are self-explanatory.

In order to use the GSE in a polygraph mode, it is best to have the subject sit directly across from the operator. The machine is facing the operator so the subject cannot see the settings or the readings on the meter. However, we found it to be beneficial to leave the volume at a degree where the subject can hear the noise made by changes in electrical response. As with any other polygraph or means of truth determining, it is necessary to establish a base line for each subject. This is done by having the subject relax and asking non-threatening incidental type questions. Within a few seconds or a minute at the most, the needle should be adjusted to rest at mid-scale and will vary no more than a few degrees in any direction with any non-threatening question. At this point the GSR is adjusted correctly and the next stage can begin.

If the volume is turned up, using the speaker, the operator and the subject will hear a steady tone, indicating the base line reading. One should allow somewhere between 10 and 30 seconds between each question. This will allow the readings to stabilize. You'll soon to able to tell how much time your subject needs between questions by watching the indicators.

Depending upon your circumstances, you may want to test out the ability of the GSR to record stress indications at this time. One way of doing so is by reaching over and simply slapping your subject. While this may not sound too kind, and is not normally done in a professional setting, the slap should bring about a full scale deviation on the meter accompanied by a very noticeable change in the tone. An anticipation of a slap, that is stopping before actual contact, should bring about the same type of reading. This is especially noticeable if it follows an actual slap.

Another thing to do is to have the subject take a deep breath and hold it. As the body requires more oxygen, a stressful condition will be produced and you will notice the meter and the tone begin to indicate stress. During this type of setup experiments or in a more professional setting by using control questions as we've discussed elsewhere that one expects a lying response to, the machine itself should be adjusted in order to give a full scale deviation of the meter during stressful situations. This makes it much easier to pick out lies or stress indicators than if the meter just deviates slightly.

This is accomplished by setting the sensitivity control following these types of questions or effects so you are sitting on a balanced mid-scale reading during normal questioning and a full-scale or off-scale deviation during stressful questioning. This sounds complicated. It's not. It's quite easy to do with this device.

Once you are ready to begin the actual experiments or tests, turn the volume up so the subject can hear the tone and begin with a number of non-relevant questions to verify your base line is indeed correct. This can include the standard: your name, where you were born, any nonsense that the subject will tell the truth on or that can be verified.

At this point, you can do a couple things. Either have the subject pick a number between one and 10 and make him or her write it down on a piece of paper, folded so you cannot see it, or have a few standard playing cards handy, have him pick a card without telling you which one it is. Obviously using a full deck wastes time so just choose ten cards and make a list of them in advance. Now you instruct your subject to answer "no" to every question you ask. If it's a number question, you begin by going, "Was it number one?" The subject replies "No". And on through ten. If you've set the device up correctly and you have a normal subject, and you reach the target number, the meter will swing to full scale, the tone will rise very audibly, and it will become very obvious to the subject that this magic machine is indicating when he's lying. This is an important setup in any polygraph test as it installs fear in the subject and a belief in the machine and the operator.

With this particular GSR we found it to be workable on every subject we used who had not been prepped or taught any deception techniques. Many subjects were amazed by this reaction and this fearfulness or anticipation adds to the response of the next series of questions, which will include any relevant questions that one wishes to establish the truthfulness of.

Once the ability of the GSR has been established, it can be extremely useful in practicing the various techniques we've outlined for polygraph deception. You can get an immediate feedback on what works and what doesn't work. While there's no guarantee that a technique that will defeat the GSR will defeat other indicators as well, it should be remembered that the GSR is usually the most sensitive and heart of any lie detector test. Therefore, it does give a fairly good reading of how your body is reacting to any situation.

It is best not to use the GSR on yourself. In other words, if you are employing it as a practical indicator of deception response and your ability to control it, have someone else operate the device while you are the subject. Experiment with this. Try all our various methods and see which one works best for you. At the very least, run through the test a number of times preparing yourself for the questions and becoming familiar with the sequence and the operation of the GSR. This will help in any sort of polygraph examination.

PHYSICAL MANIPULATION TECHNIQUES

When faced with the GSR or polygraph using a GSR, there are a number of simple physical methods that can be employed to confuse and/or defeat the purpose of the device. To start off with, one of the best we found, was to take a strong anti-perspirant. In our case we used Arid Extra Dry and sprayed it on all of the subject's fingers right before the test. It was allowed to dry and the GSR was hooked up and the sequence repeated.

This had the effect of letting us establish a base line, which appeared normal, and there was no obvious deviation during any lie. In other words, it appeared to defeat the GSR's purpose entirely. However, it should also be noted, that in this application as well as the following ones, there was no indication of a lie during the setup questions. In other words, it became impossible to find the correct number or elicit any off-scale readings for stressful questions. This could easily warn a professional operator that something is not right or that the subject is not testable. The answer to this is to try and force the reading during the lying setup so he does come out with the correct answer. This can be done by several methods as we've discussed elsewhere using a thumb tack under the toe, inducing stress as much as possible.

If one can pull off this early stress indication and then simply relax, the anti-perspirant will effectively block the secretions during the rest of the test, leaving the chart or visual indicators stable and showing no lying.

We also applied clear nail polish to the target's fingers, allowed it to dry, and repeated the sequence of tests. This produced a slightly odder base line. The sensitivity had to be turned up considerably to the point where it seemed to induce wild swings without any stressful reaction. We could not find the target number. We could not detect any lies, but the instability or the degree of sensitivity required to even establish the medium, makes it look slightly suspicious Also, it should be noted that some clear nail polishes can be seen on the skin if anyone looks for them.

We also tried something called "New Skin", which is one of the first plastics ever invented and is now used as a surrogate bandage to apply over cuts or breaks in the skin. This was even more exaggerated than the clear nail polish as it become extremely hard to stabilize the base line on normal questions. There were wild swings of the meter, there was no reaction at all to the lies or stressful indicators. Any change appeared massive. The lies would have passed as truths if a base line had been established, but again it was hard enough to establish a base line and might have tipped off an operator. If the New Skin is on the finger for very long, it becomes fairly easy to detect visually.

We also attempted to use a makeup foundation base. This did not work extremely well as it does not blend in with the skin, is noticeable, and really did not provide the resistance to change the other chemicals did.

One can experiment with this to find out one's own favorite, but the Arid actually seemed to be the best for our purposes. Again this is only going to affect the GSR portion of any polygraph and if it is coupled with the pneumatic or breathing detector, etc. In there it is not going to solve this. However, it will defeat the electrical portion of the test, making the test look invalid as somethings will indicate a deception and this particular graph will not. If it is coupled with the other methods we have gone over, it makes it much easier to establish a clean polygraph test.

In conjunction with this testing, we also went one step further than most people and we did some hypothetical experimentation on two subjects. Now please note they were hypothetical as otherwise this would be an illegal act and, of course, we didn't really do it or admit we did.; had we, and we do not advise anyone to do this in any fashion nor do we condone this action. However, hypothetically we had two subjects nasally ingest approximately three "normal" lines of high quality cocaine hydrochloride prior to the test. They were given five to ten minutes for the drug to take effect and then were tested under the same exact circumstances that they had been tested earlier without any adulterants. Surprisingly, this test seemed to be one of the most interesting. The sensitivity control had to be adjusted to almost its maximum available reading to get any reaction at all. The base line increased greatly. However, the difference or the noticeable effects, decreased greatly. There was almost no swing on the meter. The person would have passed the test with flying colors.

Again it would have been difficult to establish the initial deception in the pretesting part of the test because of this lack of sensitivity. The increased base line would not have been too serious had we not done a previous test on the same person. It would simply see the person did not sweat much and needed more sensitivity than most people.

This would not necessarily work on everyone as this is a variable, depending on the person, his psychological makeup and the strength and impurity of the drug ingested. Some people would become much more nervous and paranoid on this particular drug and establish a lower base line, but the swings still seem to be diminished in capacity and on our two subjects, the small ingestion gave them extreme confidence and a feeling that they could beat the machine. In fact, they did.

As far as we know, hypothetically speaking, we are the only people to have ever experimented on this leg of the polygraph journey. Again, we do not advise or elicit the use of any illegal act but must report it does appear this particular angle not only induces confidence in the subject, but tends to stabilize the amount of involuntary nervous system secretions and making it almost impossible "accurate" reading on a GSR type of polygraph.

It should also be noted that in many people if one passes the point of confidence by ingesting too much of this particular drug, the person may become extremely paranoid, nervous and may produce wild reaction swings on any questions that approach the stressful level. This will invalidate the test.

However, at this point it becomes fairly easy for an experienced operator to suggest the subject was using drugs, thereby in effect, proving his guilt and not exactly invalidating the test but invalidating the subject as someone not to be trusted and probably lying. This experimentation, should anyone do it, must be done with caution.

To sum up, we found the Bio Logic GSR an invaluable tool in testing any theory of polygraph deception and manual stabalization as well as an effective instrument to use on the uninitiated to detect lies. We advise the purchase of this device and subsequent use and practice to anyone who is serious about attempting to defeat the polygraph.

Of course, if one can afford four, five or six thousand dollars and wishes to buy one of the better units available, they will produce an overall better chance at deception practice as they measure more than the GSR does. However, the GSR is the heart of most polygraphs and is probably the most accurate single indication of stress or deception. If one can defeat this instrument through organic methods or physical methods, as we've detailed, chances are quite good one can transfer this same series of responses to even the more expensive polygraphs.

This GSR was not designed or ever advertised to be a polygraph, but is very sensitive, works as advertised, and will function as a reliable low-level polygraph. The device is also sold by Edmund Scientific Corporation for the same retail price.

PROJECT POLYGRAPH: THE SECRET GOVERNMENT EXPERIMENTS

The following procedures were developed by a Doctor in Psychology under contract for a certain government agency. The idea behind the project was to train certain men to defeat the polygraph in case their activities were to come under scrutiny by any "hostile" agency or government.

Here are the test results and recommendations from the Top Secret project on a word by word basis. The name of the doctor in charge as well as the other personnel involved and the actual location are all that has been changed:

"We never used drugs, as the detection of such will be construed as evidence of guilt. So would evidence of trying to foul the operation or alter responses cause the polygrapher to assume guilt.

First and foremost, all my men were "stress innoculated". By analogy, stress innoculation is essentially a "dry run". Just as men crawl under the wire while live rounds fly overhead serves to lower the adrenaline to a manageable level, so does stress innoculation for the polygraph assure the man of handling the control question EXACTLY RIGHT. And a control question handled EXACTLY RIGHT means that HIS BODY RESPONSES TO THAT CONTROL QUESTION MUST YIELD MORE SIGNIFICANT READINGS THAN HIS ACTUAL KEY ITEMS(S).

Stress innoculation for the polygraph requires that the man know what the chair looks like, that he see it physically, if at all possible, that he sit in it and that he practice his movements to get his control question exactly right. He is instructed that the polygrapher will IMPRESS HIM WITH HIS EXPERTISE, THAT THE POLYGRAPHER WILL PROUDLY DISPLAY THE TRAPPING OF HIS ROOM IN A SUBTLE MANNER IMPLYING THERE IS A "FLY-IN-THE-WEB". ALSO, BEFORE THE POLYGRAPHER BEGINS, HE MAKES INQUIRIES AIMED AT EXTRACTING A CONFESSION.

The testee must do the following:

1. Do not be overly friendly and "chatty". This is viewed as a simple con and guilt.

2. Do not be aloof and reserved. This is viewed as deep anxiety/fear, hence guilt.

3. One should be the epitome of professionalism, smile casually and appropriately.

4. And one must learn social decorum, manners and exude congeniality QUIETLY.

5. At an appropriate time, express admiration at the scientific capabilities of his instrument, adding that you have faith that it is bound to clear you of any clouds.

6. ABSOLUTELY show up <u>ahead of time</u> for your test, but do not enter the building until 15 minutes before it begins. Lateness, cancellations, illnesses ARE VIEWED VERY NEGATIVELY by correlational studies done by men such as Lykken, David.

While in the chair under controlled/known questions:

1. Prepare for being asked to think up an event within the past year about which you are quite guilty--like you stole something valuable and feel bad about it. The polygrapher will use this as his control question and assess your body's responses.

2. Make sure you come up with something that you do <u>not</u> feel guilty about but say that you do. Then when this question is asked, contract your diaphragm and gluteus maximus (butt muscles). These shoot up your blood pressure.

3. Just before giving your answer to this question, take a deep breath, hold it, then reply. This will give a "guilt" response to the control.

4. On your key question for deciding guilt/innocence, it is imperative not to get confused: DO NOT contract any muscles or hold your breath. Relax, breathe evenly, and give a firm, clear response.

5. Anticipate several runs of this.

Each of my men were put through a dozen dry runs in a chair similar to the actual. All eight of my men mastered the system such that none were ever discovered. The study was a double blind. Only I knew who had been trained. Results were put in sealed envelopes and held by Major Smith at XXX Headquarters until the tests were completed.

N.B. SOME POLYGRAPHERS ANTICIPATE THAT THIGH MUSCLES WILL BE FOILING THE CONTROL QUESTIONS, SO THEY EQUIP THE CHAIR WITH A PNEUMATIC SYSTEM. GUILT IS ASSUMED IF THIS IS DETECTED. DIAPHRAGM AND GLUTEUS/SPHINCTER AREAS (squeezing as if to get an erection or retain urine or hold bowels) are nondetectable by the pneumatic.

If one's chair has a pneumatic:

1. The testee must practice contracting the muscle groups described

above.

2. Learn, repeat, and BELIEVE that "Nothing is right or wrong, except that thinking makes it so." William Shakespeare.

3. Learn, repeat, and BELIEVE that "If you believe you can or cannot do something, you are right." Henry Ford.

There are more kinds of tests on the Poly, however, these become variations on a theme, and once one learns the above, a familiarization with the system and questions will carry one through.

Dr. John Simmons, PhD.

COUNTERMEASURES: ACTIVE

Up to now the countermeasures or counterstress procedures have been passive in nature. There are a number of much more active ways to alter the stress recording ability of any type of polygraph machine. We're going to begin looking at those. Let's start with the ones that are easier to do; that is, require less equipment and/or less chemical paraphernalia and work up to some of the more exotic methods used by the intelligence agents in the intelligence community and other professionals who have to pass polygraph examinations.

At the very beginning let's look at the effect that setting has on a polygraph test.

INSTRUMENT

Some research, reported by Orne and his colleagues, addresses the question of the situational features necessary for a polygraph examination. In one component of a study reported by Orne, et al. subjects were led to believe that the polygraph recording equipment was not operative. There was some indication that the pretest condition in which subjects were led to believe that the polygraph instrument was inoperative produced a lower detectability.

A more recent study by Orne's group tested a similar hypothesis using a different procedure. In this study, subjects saw the polygraph machine turned off, although the experimenters actually ran the leads to a second polygraph device and were able to record responses during a pretest review of questions. The results indicated that subjects who were aware of being recorded had significantly higher responses to relevant questions and not significantly different responses to control questions.

It's also been proven when subjects think they are being deceived or are overly suspicious about the examiner and/or the procedure, they may respond to the examiner's questions so erratically that no correct diagnostic opinion can be formed. In other words, if you can convince yourself that the examiner is out to deceive you or the examiner is bad enough to set out to deceive you, ask deceiving questions, or does not appear to know what he's doing with the machine, this mind-set alone can help alter the results of the examination and yields many more inconclusives than a normal testing procedure would.

From there it's a short step to practice. Yes, as in any sport, lying can be improved with practice. This has been positively proven in a number of studies, one of which we are going to take a look at right here.

Procedure

Seventy-two males participated in a study to determine the effect of information and practice on detection of deception. The 36 guilty subjects participated in a mock crime (stealing a ring). The 36 innocent subjects were told a theft had occurred. Prior to their polygraph test, subjects were divided into the following groups with 12 innocent and 12 guilty subjects in each group: (1) STD - Subjects merely waited in a room before their polygraph test, (2) INFO - Subjects were given information about the nature of the polygraph and how to appear innocent, and (3) INFO + Practice - Subjects were given the same information as group two, and two polygraph practice sessions with feedback about their performance. Examiners (not professional polygraph examiners), blind to a subject's guilt or innocence, administered a control question polygraph test. Subjects were paid $7.50 for participating in the study and $10 if the outcome of their test was truthful. All subjects were to deny involvement in the theft. Skin conductance, blood pressure, respiration, and digital vasomotor activity were recorded; there were three charts per subject. Responses were scored with a numerical scoring system and an inconclusive range of plus or minus five. Results are based on the scoring of a second examiner blind to test results and subject status.

Results

INFO + Practice reduced the number of correct classifications and increased the number of false positives and negatives. That is, 62.5% were correctly classified, 25% were incorrectly classified (three false positives and three false negatives), and 12.5% were inconclusive. Analysis of variance and post-hoc comparisons revealed that the innocent subjects in the INFO + Practice group had significantly lower scores than the other two groups.

Some time ago the CIA, concerned with the possibility of operatives encountering a polygraph examination when attempting to infiltrate a target group, conducted a detailed study on the accuracy of the device in several settings. A summary of their tests is important to our study:

The CIA testing was divided into three sets: the first set was conducted in conjunction with a sheriff's office when they were screening applicants for an opening in their department. The results, in terms of admissions, inferred lies, and operator suggestions for hiring were compared to a study of other selection procedures including initial interview, background and document tests, etc. It was found that the polygraph operator's report yielded information not shown by the other devices, information with a high probably relevance to final decisions to hire or not to hire. ALMOST ALL VALUABLE POLYGRAPH INFORMATION WAS DERIVED FROM ADMISSIONS from the subjects. There was no evidence, from that study, of the utility of the polygraph in applicant selection EXCEPT when the subject made admissions.

One possibility raised by this test was that the examination yielded up indiscreet men for rejection, but did not find adverse information on a man careful enough to conceal misbehavior from all selection devices and wise enough to make no admissions during the polygraph examination. In an effort to test the utility of the device in a setting where no admissions would be allowed, a second study was undertaken.

In the second study, the subjects used were reliable police informants. Some of the subjects were to repeat a story that had proven out under investigation. A second group was instructed to tell a true story, but to insert several crucial points of misinformation, while a third group told stories appropriate to the informant's situation, but which were incorrect in all points necessary to the police. The polygraph operators were to identify correct/incorrect stories as well as the correct/incorrect points within the story.

All true stories were correctly identified as such and all stories containing one or more false items were correctly chosen as containing false items. This association between polygraph operator judgment and the overall true/false content was excellent. A few errors were made within the stories in discriminating the truth and falseness of separate items; of a total of 106 items, 102 were correctly identified as true or false, and 4 were incorrectly identified.

This tends to substantiate the polygraph examination under conditions where admissions and confessions do not occur. Still, certain doubts remain. All the informants were "tame", they had volunteered to tell information to the police and all were "truth tellers". It is possible that situations and experimenters can elicit biased behavior among subjects, there was also the possibility that the cooperative informants had been physiologically convinced or had otherwise given clues to the examiner.

The third experiment was the most viable; a group of 13 adult males (civilian) and 24 male police officers were chosen for this test. All the police officers had experience working undercover in assignments that required consistent and effective deception of those around them.

Each subject was told the purpose of the test was only to see how well they could "beat the box". Subjects were told they would be paid for their time, and in addition, given a bonus if they could deceive the machine. Each was explained the general format of the test; that all would be posing as civilians and presenting either real or false stories. The task of the polygraph operator was to differentiate the genuine officers from the civilians.

Prior to the examination each officer was asked to develop a civilian autobiography that he felt comfortable with. The elements of the story were agreed upon and written down. (A civilian actor was hired and given the same task, but during the pre-test he became so upset he forgot his story and confessed to the truth).

The examiner was restricted to six questions plus two control questions. The questions were: Were you actually born in XXXXX? Did you ever engage in any law enforcement work? Did you ever engage in any undercover investigation work? Were you actually born on XXXXX? Are you concealing any information about your parents? Did you lie to any questions on this test?

All subjects were instructed to say "no" to the control questions: Did anyone help you prepare for this test? Did you plan with anyone to lie on this test?

Each subject completed a fact sheet about his life and work history. Civilians were instructed to tell the truth during the examination and the undercover cops were told not to "cop out" under any circumstances. That is, not to be persuaded to tell the truth on any lie item.

The officers were then divided into two groups; one group of 12 men received a briefing on what would happen during the test. These men were "rehearsed" on their stories by another polygraph examiner for one to two hours and shown the polygraph. The second group received no briefing.

The examination took one hour. In addition to the pre-polygraph interview and the examination, the examiner was allowed to search coats left hanging in the observation room.

After the examination, the examiner labeled each response as truth or a lie or "doubtful". It should be noted that the examiner had a definite psychological advantage, as he knew the nature of the experiment and would guess that at least half of the subjects were undercover officers.   This is the reasoning behind the weighted (24-13) ratio of cops to civilians.

The results of the experiment are quite interesting:

Overall - Out of 95 lies, 72 were correctly detected, giving a batting average of 76%. Out of 128 truthful items 61 (48%) were correctly identified.

Subgrouping - 34 out of 42 lies (81%) were identified in the unbriefed police group, compared with 38 out of 53 (72%) in the trained sample. Truthful statements accepted were 46 out of 78 (59%) in the civilian group, 9 out of 30 (30%) in the untrained police group, and 5 out of 19 (37%) in the briefed police group.

In a broad view, how did the examiner perform with regard to persons, rather than statements? In effect, if any statement labeled a lie would make a subject suspect for purposes of employment, how many would have passed?

	One or more replies labeled lies	No lies, one or more doubtful	No lies, no doubtfuls
Civilians	10	2	1
Unbrief Cops	11	1	0
Brief Cops	11	1	0

The doubtful judgments represent inconclusive findings from the examiners standpoint. If one assumes that inconclusive findings were NOT to be considered "Suspect" (that is, they passed) three out of the 13 civilians would have been labeled as okay for hiring... It also means that two out of 24 officers, who were, in fact, lying, would also be considered acceptable.

What one finds is a rate of false positives of 10/13, that is, 10 rejected who should have been accepted and a 2/24 rate of false negatives, that is, persons accepted who should have been rejected.

If, on the other hand, "doubtful" replies ARE considered suspect, meaning they too would be rejected, the rate of false positives for civilians rises to 12 out of 13 and the false negatives among officers drops to 0 out of 24. Thus, all the lying cops would have been screened out, although almost all the honest civilians would have also been rejected.

It is obvious that either approach for the identification of liars is unworkable in most practicable employment applications because most truth tellers would be rejected along with the liars. One would conclude that the polygraph examination used in this way, and under the unusual "no cop out" rule, would provide little benefit as a screening device. But, let's interpret a bit deeper:

Among the six questions were two "critical" to this test --"Did you ever engage in any undercover work?" and "Did you ever engage in any law enforcement work?" These two questions are the core of the examination since the examiner was attempting to identify the liars, all of whom had to lie on these questions.

If we concentrate on these two questions, the entire emphasis shifts; it is important to understand in some cases, depending on personnel policies, number of job applicants, etc., a "doubtful" or "inclusive" result could be judged either way.

If we consider doubtfuls to be examiner successes (more favorable conditions for the examiner) and the case of only one key lie being detected, we have a perfect score in discovering all 24 officers as lying, while two of the 13 civilians will have neither of the two key truths accepted.

If we arbitrarily consider the "doubtfuls" as lie judgments, and classify the case of one out of two lies detected as being judged truth tellers, we come up with three civilians being judged liars and 10 as truth tellers, 23 cops being judged liars and one passing as a "truthful" civilian.

In this case of considering the two key questions, we have a high ratio of the examiner being able to distinguish between the undercover officers and the civilians.

RECOMMENDATIONS FOR POLYGRAPH PRACTICE

Considering the findings above, the obvious implication is that a screening policy should limit itself to examiner judgments on two key questions only, and consider "doubtfuls" as lies-in-fact. This would be optimal for identifying deceivers of the kind who were subjects in this study. Using this policy, one would have identified 23 out of 24 officers (or 24/24 using one key statement correctly identified as a lie). One would have accepted 10 out of 13 civilians, losing three "honest" applicants incorrectly identified as liars. This encourages the theory of many polygraph operators in that the direct polygraph examination, as opposed to the pre-examination admission handles a circumscribed area of inquiry.

Under this test, when the inquiry expands even slightly to cover matters of life history, the rate of false positives rises so rapidly that almost no applicants would pass as honest. The only alternative in this broad examination would be to consider the "doubtful" statements as truths; this would give us three of the 13 "honest" civilians, but also hire two of the 24 liars. In other words, a no-cop out situation with a broad approach, we would hire almost as many liars as honest applicants.

Another sidelight of the experiment was to ascertain certain attitudes and experience as an aid to deception. With this in mind, the subjects were put through several psychological tests as well as asked questions regarding their background, whether they felt they could beat the lie detector, etc. The officers were also given the choice of telling the truth on the four life history questions and only lying on the two key questions, or lying on all six. Oddly enough, the psychological testing failed to show any particular personality traits which helped the liars, but the questionnaires they filled out did.

NEVER COP OUT. This should be obvious, yet it is one of the most frequent method of identifying liars. Remember, the applicant has nothing to lose by lying, except being branded a liar.

BE CONFIDENT. Two items were significantly related to being a better or worse liar, within the questions asked each officer. Quite simply, the better liars SAID they were good liars. Also, the better liars said they expected to beat the polygraph. The worse liars were not sure, or did not expect to beat it. No other conceptions about lying, ambivalence, years of undercover work, etc., had any effect on the ability to lie.

LIE OFTEN. Out of the people who told five or six lies on the test, eight were among the best liars and one was in the worse group. Of people who told four or less, three were better and 12 were in the worse group. One concludes that the more lies one tells, the greater chance of being a better liar.

Another advantage to lying often is that the officers lying on the key points stood out more and had a greater vulnerability to the examiner, where the liars who lied on the life history events, as well, enjoyed the advantages of a diffused effort by the examiner.

ONE OF THE INHERENT DANGERS OF THE LIE DETECTOR IS THE FALSE POSITIVE SYNDROME. In the CIA tests, only one man out of 34 had all his truthful statements accepted as such. Discarding the three officers who lied on all six questions, 18 men had more than HALF THEIR TRUTHFUL STATEMENTS LABELED AS LIES.

A "halo" effect was also deduced; i.e., when the examiner noted lying on a key question, he tended to consider statements other than the replies to these questions lies also.

CONCLUSIONS

From the foregoing studies and research, it is obvious that practice, familiarization, learning to relax, learning to apply the right mind-set techniques can greatly alter the outcome of any polygraph test. Just as in a kinesic interview, knowing what you are dealing with, knowing what questions to recognize, what does what, and how to control it may solve the problem of the polygraph test for a number of people. Now this won't work with everyone, but it is a very good start and something very important to work on.

The only problem with this method is lack of feedback. It would be ideal to have a polygraph instrument at your disposal and, preferably an operator, to test out your daily progress in practicing. Unfortunately, this is prohibitively expensive for most of us. There are, however, a couple of other alternatives, mechanical means for feedback on some of the same measurements, measuring modes that the polygraph uses. We will get into them at the end of this chapter on "mechanical means" as these mechanical feedback devices will work on all our countermeasures, not just the practice mind-set techniques.

HYPNOSIS/ BIO-FEEDBACK

There is a substantial literature in psychology about the use of hypnosis and biofeedback to alter and condition physiological responses. There is some evidence that hypnosis, for example, induces declines in skin conductance levels.

Recent research by Corcoran, Lewis, and Garver has examined the effects of biofeedback training on suppressing EDR. They found that both hypnosis and biofeedback groups were able to reduce detectability after training as compared to a control group. Information about the nature of lie detection and practice using countermeasures were detected significantly less than subjects without such training. It seems clear that if hypnosis or biofeedback operate as countermeasures, especially with commonly used tests such as CQT, extensive training would have to accompany their use

MENTAL

Another category of countermeasures involves those that get the subject to think differently about the test. As noted earlier, most polygraph examinations rely on the subject's motivation to avoid detection rather than on any response directly connected with "telling a lie." Simple cognitive countermeasures include patterns of thinking that suppress responses to control or irrelevant questions. More complex cognitive countermeasures are based on knowledge of the results of the examination and lack of belief in one's detectability.

CONTROLLING THOUGHTS

Any individual who understands the basic structure of a particular polygraph examination should be able to differentiate irrelevant and control from relevant questions (when an R/I or CQT examination is conducted). Given that when a CQT is employed, the questions are reviewed prior to their presentation, a subject intent on deception could try to alter cognitively responses to various questions (although, since the order of presentation is varied, this is made difficult during an actual test). The procedure would be to try to dissociate oneself from the relevant questions and heighten response to control questions. Various means of such mental dissociation have been described. They range from concentrating on an irrelevant object or by convincing oneself that the question means something different than intended.

KNOWLEDGE OF RESULTS

Another set of countermeasures is based on subjects having knowledge of the results of their polygraph examination. In criminal situations, particularly when an inconclusive outcome is obtained or when the subject disagrees with the outcome of an initial polygraph test, subjects are retested. In noncriminal situations, individuals are often tested at the beginning of their employment and at a number of subsequent points. In addition, subjects who know that they will receive a polygraph examination may seek training in methods to avoid detection. For all of these reasons, it is important to understand how feedback about polygraph examinations affects validity and whether prior experiences represent a potential countermeasure.

In an early laboratory study, subjects were given a stimulation test and feedback concerning its outcome. Feedback was manipulated so that some subjects thought they had successfully avoided detection and others thought that they had not. Subjects were motivated on a subsequent trial to avoid detection (they were told, "only nature and stable individuals are able to fool the lie detector"). The results indicated that subjects who believed that they had avoided detection were much less detectable on the second trial (13 out of 16 were not detected, while only one of 16 in a control group were able to avoid detection). It should be noted that a stimulation test is a form of a concealed information test and the result may be due to lowered overall arousal. "Beating" a CQT represents a somewhat different problem.

A recent study, by Rovner, et al., tested a similar hypothesis in a CQT examination. Several groups of subjects were placed in a mock crime situation. One group was given information about the nature of a CQT examination and information on what physiological reactions they would try to simulate. Another group was given information plus two practice tests involving actual physiological recordings after which they were told whether or not they had beat the polygraph. A third group served as a control and was given a typical polygraph examination. The results indicated that the information only and control group were not able to avoid detection; however, 25 percent of the guilty subjects in the information plus practice group were able to avoid detection.

COUNTERMEASURES ACTIVE: CHEMICAL

In the last few years a number of groups have become concerned with the possible effects of various chemicals on the polygraph and PSE type testing procedures. Both the government, private lie detector organizations, universities and our trusty, little staff have done tests which have brought some very interesting conclusions. We are going to begin studying these chemical altering agents by looking at a couple general rules: First of all, these agents are in three or four definite medical groups and it is important to understand a little bit about each group before even thinking of the possibility of indulging, or if you are an examiner, the possibility of the person you are examining having indulged in any of these chemical changers.

We must say that under no circumstances do we recommend, suggest or take any responsibility for anyone taking any sort of drug, prescribed or otherwise, especially drugs nonprescribed for them. Also, we take no responsibility but point out the fact if someone takes a drug not prescribed for them (a prescription drug), it is wise to take the drug several times in advance of the actual crucial period to establish what side effects, if any, and what results may entail from the drug's ingestion. Failure to do this can cause severe consequences.

To begin with, we are going to start with some of the later research on fairly new drugs that seem to have a definite effect on polygraphic detection of deception or lies. One of these drugs is known as propranolol. This is the generic name; the drug is normally sold under the name of Inderal and is prescribed for hypertension or high blood pressure. This is the usual prescription. The drug has an interesting side effect which is known in the medical profession, although not listed in the books and not officially prescribed for, as a cure-all for stage fright. People who are professional lecturers or have an important business engagement at which they must give a speech before a large number of people, can sometimes talk a friendly physical into prescribing a small amount of Inderal for this occasion to combat the stomach butterflies, the common tendency we call stage fright. PDR, the *Physicans' Desk Reference*, does not list Inderal for this purpose, but it has been known to be prescribed for this. Generally it is prescribed only for hypertension or high blood pressure.

The way propranolol works is it blocks certain cells' beta reception in the autonomic nervous system. That is, it reduces the transmission of the fight or flight syndrome and thereby reduces tension and excitation to both the normal and the autonomic nervous system. This in turn tends to lower blood pressure, tends to even out the reaction peaks to any sort of excitation syndrome. It tends to fight the tension that normally occurs during an emergency or pressure situation, both in a physiological and psychological manner, although more so in a physiological manner.

This drug is not a central nervous system depressant nor is it a tranquilizer. It is a beta blocking drug which tends to block the inner action of synapse responses to tension or excitation, which results in a more even and lower pulse and blood pressure rate. It is very effective in polygraph and PSE type deceptions because of this exact factor. The drug is normally given in approximately 40 milligram doses. Taking more of the drug does not seem to increase the beta blocking effect, and on the other hand, can cause a dangerous overdose situation. We do not recommend taking this drug under any circumstances except for its prescribed purpose; that is to combat hypertension when given by a doctor.

However, there have been a number of tests inspired by Inderal or propranolol on the polygraph that have some interesting results. We are going to reproduce one test here that was done about four years ago in a paper presented to a science group on the effects of propranolol on the detection of deception.

PROCEDURE

Twenty-eight males aged 20 to 40 years were paid $15 for participating in a study to determine the effect of propranolol on detection of deception in a mock crime situation. Subjects were randomly assigned to one of four groups (seven subjects per group); (1) Guilty - propranolol, (2) Guilty - no propranolol; (3) Innocent - propranolol, and (4) Innocent - no propranolol. The guilty subjects were required to steal and then hide a piece of jewelry from an office in one hour. Innocent subjects were told that a mock crime had taken place but were not told details. All subjects were told to deny involvement in the crime. Both innocent and guilty subjects could receive a $10 bonus for appearing truthful on the test. Drug subjects received a 40 mg. tablet of propranolol one to two hours before the polygraph test.

Blood pressure, electrodermal activity, and abdominal and thoracic respiration were recorded. Two professional polygraph examiners (each testing 14 subjects), blind to subject's assigned group status, administered a nine-item control question polygraph test. Detection was based on pairs of control-relevant questions (the last six questions). Each pair was scored (by the examiner) from +3 to -3 based on the size of the relative difference. Respiration was scored based on the clearest channel. Scores were summed across pairs and channels. Subjects with score +6 or higher were designated truthful, -6 or lower were designated as deceptive, and inconclusive between plus or minus 5. Examiners also rated on a seven-point scale whether they thought the subject had taken a drug.

There was a definite difference in the group that took the drug from the placebo and other test group. The fact that the correct classification was significantly reduced and many more passed as innocent that were guilty, is interesting and important to realize that in most of these tests, the examiner is informed a drug is involved and inconclusives again are thrown out, which would have greatly raised the score to almost 100% status of passing if you took the inconclusives as failures to detect and also puts the examiner on his toes to watch for certain symbols that he would not otherwise be watching for. This is a very interesting drug.

In one other test, which we are not going to quote in full, but also is a substantial test by a well-known group who did this to study deception, 100% of the people who took the propranolol that were guilty were classified as innocent. Note that again--100% were classified as innocent. In our own test with this drug we have ranged between, without telling the examiner that a drug test was occurring, and including inconclusives in the test results, a 75 --100% deception rate.

It should be noted this is a fairly short-acting drug. Peak effect occurs in one to one and a half hours after ingestion, depending on the stomach contents, etc. Empty stomachs tend to encourage early drug come-on effects and have life for approximately two to three hours, so it is a drug that needs to be taken near the test and should be tested on the individual before any attempts are made to use it as a beta blocking agent or edonomic nervous system controller for polygraph purposes. However, it does work.

Another beta blocking drug known as Tenormin or atenolol is also a possible candidate for this type of polygraphic deception. It, too, is a beta blocking agent, although of a longer lasting variety. In fact, tenormin normally is taken only once in a 24-hour period for hypertension and peak levels are reached between two and four hours after ingestion. It undergoes a different metabolism process than does Inderal and may not be as effective. It is never, or to our knowledge, ever prescribed as a stage fright combatant drug but strictly as a hypertension agent and achieves this hypertension reduction by blocking the beta cell receptors as does propranolol from excitation syndrome. It would have some effect on a polygraph test, although the test results we did rather informally, showed it was not nearly as effective as propranolol. However, it does have some beta blocking effect and can establish more inconclusives and does allow occasional guilty to pass as innocent.

The second drug we need to look at is a drug known as meprobamate. This is the generic name. The common names are Miltown or Equanil. This is a different classification of drug all together. This is one of the minor tranquilizers, as in Valium, etc., and is an anxiety combatant and CNS (entral nevous system) depressant. In other words it reduces activities in certain areas of the brain thought to effect emotional and autonomic nervous system responses. Again, it fights the fight or flight syndrome.

Miltown or Equanil is prescribed to people by doctors because they are nervous, anxiety ridden, or have trouble sleeping, although it is not a sleeping pill. It can produce sleepiness. It is also necessary to note that any CNS type depressant has usually cross tolerance with alcohol and will increase itself logarithmically with a couple shots of booze. This is not a good idea unless you have tried it in advance. It is NEVER a good idea according to the Federal Drug Administration or the *Physicans' Desk Reference.* It may cause the side effects to become more apparent than the actual effect of the drug.

Miltown has had some interesting publicity in regard to lie detectors in the last year or so. One test on college students, we're going to repeat right here. They were given 400 milligrams of meprobamate.

PROCEDURE

Male college students (aged 18 to 24 years) were paid $2 an hour as subjects in an experiment to determine the effect of meprobamate on detection of deception. Subjects designated guilty overlearned six words during time, interpreted tasks prior to the polygraph test. Innocent subjects performed the same tasks but learned no words. Guilty subjects were told that it was possible to deceive the examiner, whereas innocent subjects were told it is often difficult to prove one's innocence. Guilty subjects were randomly assigned to one of three groups (11 per group). One group was told they were taking a tranquilizer which would help them avoid detection and were given 400 mg. meprobamate. Another group was given a placebo. The third guilty group received nothing.

After 30 minutes, a second experimenter, blind to subject status, administered a polygraph test using the guilty knowledge technique. The question list consisted of 24 words, four in each of six categories. One of the four words in each category was a word the guilty subject memorized. The first word of the list was a dummy word. The list was presented twice. The examiner also completed a rating scale about his perception of subject's drug status.

Electrodermal response amplitude, smallest inspiration, and change in relative blood pressure were recorded and scored by technicians who had not observed the test. A subject was classified guilty if his response to the relevant word in each set of four produced a larger response than the remaining three words on five or more sets. In order to analyze data from innocent subjects, one word in each set of four was randomly designated as the critical word.

Correct classification was reduced significantly in the meprobamate group.

In another test done by a lie detector agency the guilty subjects, using a control zone question type test, were including inconclusives almost 100% passable on Miltown. Now in this test, the lie detector examiner, the polygraph operator, did not know the subjects had been using a drug. The inconclusives were greater. The percentage of passage was excellent. In our own tests we found Miltown to be as effective or more effective than Inderal.

The problem is there are some side effects with Miltown as there are with any minor tranquilizers or CNS depressants and possibly a good polygraph operator would catch these side effects. Note our chart which is a standard chart published for polygraph operators to look for side effects that may come through drug usage during the test. Beta blocking drugs, such as propranolol and tenormin do not produce these side effects in the least. Miltown and meprobamate may be a small bit more effective, but they may produce side effects and one must test first to see if these side effects are there before attempting to use them for any polygraphic- prophylatic type purpose. Miltown does increase its effectiveness with the amount of dosage up to a certain point where a borderline is crossed and it becomes dangerous and is often prescribed in 600 milligram dosages rather than the 400 milligrams used in the first test. We found that 600 milligrams does make a difference.

There are two other drugs rarely ever mentioned, called Solazine and Tybatran that are both similar to meprobamate in action and would probably also serve in this regard, although we did not run tests on them. These are again minor tranquilizers, central nervous system depressants that are prescribed as anti-anxiety agents. In other words they stop the fight or flight syndrome. They stop the excitation tension resulting from an anxiety-written situation. These two drugs are normally given in 500 - 1500 milligram dosages and the higher dosages would probably produce more of the effects that would be beneficial to anyone trying to deceive a polygraph or PSE machine.

Another drug that has been successfully used at time for prophylatic effects on polygraph machines is Valium. This is the most common drug prescribed in America as I write this. It is an anti-anxiety, anti-depressant drug that is not supposed to cause sleep but does reduce physical and emotional responses to stress. It has an amazing cross tolerance with alcohol and should not be taken with it. Heavy equipment should not be operated, etc. It is a prescription drug, but as I have said, it is the most prescribed drug in America right now. There are some side effects that a trained observer, please refer to the chart, can often spot in the user of Valium. Valium has been around for years. The generic name is diazepam and it's a Roche drug. It is found to have cardiovascular depressor effects in experiments. A normal dose ranges from two milligrams through 10 milligrams at one time. Again, this is a rather heavy C even though it is classified as a minor tranquilizer. It is a rather heavy CNS depressant and should never be taken without prior knowledge of its effects on a certain human being because it is likely to leave side effects apparent to a good operator.

Tests results on Valium differ. According to the Department of Defense it has almost no response or efficiency in defeating the polygraph machine. However, we're going to reprint a small test done by Lee Lapin in which Valium was found to be fairly effective. This again would depend on operator interpretation, if the operator knew the subjects might be on drugs, and type of questions and question test used. Valium has a primary response in the cardiovascular and some of the pneumatic system area. If this was coupled with the GSR defusion method that we'll go into shortly, there is a chance Valium would be a much better bet at defeating the polygraph than it would be when used alone.

Another drug used to attempt to defeat the lie detector is flurazepam. This is the generic name. The normal name is Dalmane. This is somewhat of a first effect Valium. It is a cousin to Valium. However, it is more of a hypnotic drug and usually prescribed as a sleeping pill rather than as an anti-anxiety agent. It's more of a sedative and will have more of a sleep effect than a calming effect. It does not appear to be as effective as Valium in our tests in deceiving lie detectors and does produce significantly more side effects and probably should be avoided unless there's no other choice. Speaking hypothetically, of course, we do not suggest that you take any of these drugs. These are for study or research purposes only.

Now just as Valium could be considered a new and improved (in Madison Avenue lingo) version of Dalmane, there's a brand new drug out called Ativen which is generically known as lorazepam. This is another anti-anxiety drug, prescribed like Valium, but is newer and "improved" than Valium as it has different and sometimes lesser side effects. The drug is prescribed in two different ways. It is given in oral dosages of two - four milligrams to produce sedation, drowsiness or to relieve anxiety about a particular event.

It has a very interesting side effect. The side effect, it should be noted, does not occur nearly as often as when the drug is ingested. That is when it is swallowed and put into the body through the stomach walls, but is almost always present when injected in an IM sense or IV sense by a doctor or a nurse, and this side effect is that it produces temporary amnesia. Unfortunately, it is not a selective amnesia wherein one can go back and raise events from one's past, but rather produces an amensia-like state during the time the drug is used, about events currently happening. The advantage to this is the drug is often prescribed to patients undergoing an anxiety-producing surgery, wherein the doctor and the patient do not particularly want to recall the surgery afterwards. Perhaps the surgery is the type using only a local anesthetic and is going to be very gory and will leave a lasting and possibly damaging effect on the patient. Perhaps the patient is just anxiety-stricken by the hospital. When injected this drug not only produces anti-anxiety, controlling the autonomic nervous system somewhat, also producing some of the same side effects as Valium, although in a lesser state, it can produce an amnesia-like response where the patient refuses to recall or cannot recall to be more specific, the events that occurred while under the influence of this drug.

This is a very interesting drug. It's fairly hard to get a prescription for it as I write this because it's new, but like any other drug, the drug companies are going to push it heavily with their literature and probably will soon claim that it works better than Valium. You will see more and more of it on the marketplace in the next few months to a year, I would hazard a guess. This is an interesting drug which we did not test personally with a polygraph machine, but it would appear to have some definite possibilities for prophylactic effects with a polygraph or PSE machine.

Another drug occasionally used in the attempts to defeat the polygraph is Thorazine. Thorozine it should be noted, is not a minor tranquillizer, it is a MAJOR tranquillizer. The precise mechanism where the effects of thorozine, or as it is generically known, choropromazine are not exactly understood. It is available and injectable in oral form and frankly is what they give to mental patients who cannot be controlled by any other means. It produces very heavy side effects, including dopiness, dumbness, lack of motor coordination, and sleepiness. It is not recommended by the author of this book in any experiments by qualified doctors or other medical personnel because of the side effects and the general depressing effect of the drug.

This same warning can be held with almost all barbiturates. The side-producing dizziness, drowsiness, shortness of breath, slurred speech and obvious side effects, really do not seem to have much effect on the polygraph except to lower the overall baseline response, and leaves the peaks in almost the same place. Thereby this does not really make any effect on the overall outcome except perhaps an occasional inconclusive, although the obviousness of the drug almost overrides any attempt at an inconclusive reading.

Another strange drug is known as Elavil or amitriptylinehcl hydrocloride. This is a tricyclic anti-depressant. It has a strange response which can be very different on different people. It is given occasionally for an anti-depressant drug, for a sleeping drug, to prevent or reduce the obvious effects of schizophrenia. However, in some patients it does the opposite wherein it will increase the symptoms of schizophrenia and/or psychosis and may actually act as a speedy type agent rather than a depressant agent. This is a very risky drug which we do not advise any one to take except if it has been prescribed for them and they've tried it several times and understand the possible side effects and/or tested it on a mechanical feedback means, as we'll get into, for polygraph purposes.

It is possible to impair many mental or physical abilities with this drug. It may become difficult to drive, it has a high cross tolerance with alcohol and although it is classified as an anti-depressant with sedative effects, it actually can be even considered a depressant in some people. Please note this drug should NEVER be taken with MAO (monoamine oxidase) inhibitors because it can produce severe convulsions, even death unless the MAO inhibitors are completely out of the body, which is a 14 day period.

It should be noted some drugs, legal and illegal such as cocaine, are MAO inhibitors and this drug has a bad cross tolerance with them. Be careful of Elavil. We are reprinting one study, again done by Mr. Lapin, which shows elavil has an effect on polygraph techniques, but we do not advise it as a primary choice in any experimentation.

Librium, another minor tranquillizer, generically known as chlordiazepoxide is a pre-Valium tranquillizer, minor, that also produces an anti-depressant, anti-anxiety effect and can produce the same side effects as Valium. Frankly most researchers, unfortunately myself included, have found this drug to be of little or no use regardless of its reputation in polygraph examinations and would advise the avoidance of it.

Alcohol has also been advised as a possible way to defeat the polygraph. In both my tests and tests conducted by a well known group of scientists on alcohol and psychological detection and deception, we found it not to be very good. In the first place, the examiners can normally pick out the alcohol condition of the intoxicated subjects and also the only thing it seems to help on is the pneumatic measurement in guilty knowledge test.

When used in control zone question test and when lumped together with other indications, it does not seem to help much. It is possible alcohol coupled with a GSR mechanical defusion device or possibly even intermixed, although we do not advise this as this is strictly for research purposes, with a minor tranquilizer or beta blocker which has actually very little cross tolerance with alcohol, could help an individual in most types of polygraph examinations. However, this again differs greatly from subject to subject and test to test and operator to operator. Alcohol should not be considered a good way to defeat a polygraph or PSE machine.

In conclusion it should be seen that it is increasingly possible to tranquilize the polygraph. That is to beat most types of polygraph examinations with the correct chemical or correct chemical combination in one's blood stream. The two top ones are Miltown and Inderal. If one has access to these drugs and one has tested these drugs to ascertain the side effects possible prior to any testing procedures.

The individuals who are more likely to show side effects are drug abusers who take larger than normal does and subjects who take an extra dose right before an exam. The subject who takes a normal dose of these drugs tends to slip by and tends to pass the detection test. Is important, if you are a lie detector operator, to become familiar with the side effects of these drugs as we've spelled them out and as the chart shows and also if you are engaged in the research project to beat the polygraph. It is important to also to note these side effects and have an unquestioned observer tell if you are exhibiting these side effects and/or videotaping oneself while trying mechanical feedback means to ascertain if the side effects are there and if the drugs are working.

A good examiner will look for an unresponsive chart and a flat GSR reading that may indicate drugs. However, he can not prove this without a blood test and at   best will only make this an inconclusive report, especially without the accompanying side effects. An inconclusive in many cases is as good as being a pass.

The problem with drugs is they do not respond to the critical control portions of the test only, but tend to lower the response on all questions so the type of the test, the examiner, and the drug itself due to have an effect on the test and on the pass-fail percentages. It is also possible to couple, of course, drugs with knowledge of the test, practice and mechanical means to produce higher responses in control questions themselves and lower responses in peak of tension or non-control questions thereby giving a passable lie detector test. It also should be noted that these will work on the PSE as well, if not better than a lie detector.

DRUG EFFECTS

Polygraph operators are trained to watch for the following drug side effects:

meprobamate (Miltown)
  Frequent: drowsiness
  Less frequent: slurred speech

chlordiazepoxide (Librium)
  Frequent: clumsiness, drowsiness, light-headedness
  Less frequent: tiredness

diazepam (Valium)
  Frequent: clumsiness, drowsiness, tiredness
  Less frequent: lightheadedness, slurred speech

flurazepam (Dalmane)
  Frequent: drowsiness, clumsiness, dizziness
  Less frequent: slurred speech, tiredness

chloropromazine (Thorazine)
  Frequent: trembling, drowsiness, fast heartbeat, dry mouth

barbiturates
  Frequent: dizziness, drowsiness
  Less frequent: shortness of breath, tiredness, slurred speech

cocaine
  (Note most technicans are NOT yet aware of the effects of this drug)
  Frequent: rapid heart beat, hurried speech, nervous

COUNTERMEASURES: ACTIVE, PHYSICAL

There are a number of actual physical countermeasures that can be employed by a person attempting to pass or confuse a lie detector, PSE, or polygraph exam. These range from mechanical, physical devices and procedures to a use of a number of drugs, which have been recently researched and found to create significant effects in polygraph and voice stress analyzer results.

First of all, let's take a look at the pure physicals:

Physical measures taken by a subject during a polygraph examination are, perhaps, the most frequently discussed countermeasures used by subjects. Any physical activity which could affect physiological response is a potential problem for interpretation of a polygraph test record. There is no question that physical measures, from tensing muscles to biting the tongue, to squeezing toes, to shifting one's position can affect physiological response.

Kubis found that when subjects press their toes towards the floor they were able to reduce the probability of detection from 75 to 10 percent. In two more studies by Honts and Hodes, the efficacy of two physical countermeasures was tested in analog situations. Both studies found that countermeasures allowed subjects to "beat" the polygraph. Furthermore, there were a large percentage of inconclusives. In addition, both studies found that experienced examiners were not able to detect use of the countermeasures. A recent study by Honts, Raskin and Kircher also found that the use of physical countermeasures decreased detectability; cological agents have the potential to produce incorrect or uninterruptable polygraph records.

There are ways in which one can augment one's autonomic reactions to control questions. Tensing toes, tensing abdominal muscles, biting the tongue or even hiding a tack in one's sock and then pressing down on it at the appropriate times, will produce erratic polygraph readings. Once you can identify control questions, these techniques can be used to enhance the response or that is, to raise the baseline of these control questions, thereby making the baseline erratic or at least raising the baseline so the non-control or peak of tension questions will not appear to be lies, or at the very least, give inconclusive readings.

In fact, if the enhanced control responses are about equal to the responses that are guilty or stress responses to the critical questions, they must be scored as inconclusive. If the control responses are actually larger, they must be scored as truthful. Again it is nice to have feedback on these techniques. On the other hand, you have nothing to lose if you take a test and try them. Read the end of the chapter on mechanical means of getting some feedback.

SHORT GUIDE TO POLYGRAPH ADMISSIBILITY

JURISDICTION

U.S. Supreme Court
> Has refused certiorari on all cases of admissibility and denial of admissibility

First Circuit
> No positive appellate decision
>> Probably at trial judge's discretion

Second Circuit
> *Once or more admitted over objection
> No positive appellate decision
>> See admission over objection of test of witness, denial of admission of tests of defendants in U.S. v. Hart 344 F. Supp. 522 (E.D. N.Y. 1971)

Third Circuit
> No positive appellate decision

Fourth Circuit
> *Once or more admitted over objection
> No positive appellate decision
>> Admissibility probably at judge's discretion

Fifth Circuit
> Has not been admitted
>> Polygraph screening examinations do not require validation under Title VII of Civil Rights Act

Sixth Circuit
> Has been admitted on stipulations
>> Trial judge's discretion - U.S. v. Mayes 512 F. 2d 637 (1974)

Seventh Circuit
> Has been admitted on stipulations
>> Admissibility at judge's discretion - U.S. v. Inflice 506 F. 2d 1358 (1974)

Eighth Circuit

Has been admitted on stipulations
U.S. v. Earley 657 F. 2d 195 (1981)

Ninth Circuit
Has been admitted on stipulations
Herman v. Eagle Star Insurance Co., 396 F. 2d 427 (1968)

Tenth Circuit
Has not been admitted
Chavez v. State of New Mexico, 456 F. 2d 1073 (1972)

Eleventh Circuit
No positive appellate decision
Jones v. Weldon, 690 F. 2d 835 (1982)

District of Columbia Circuit
Has not been admitted
Frye v. U.S., 54 App. D.C. 46, 293 F. 1013 (1923)

Alabama
Has been admitted on stipulations

Alaska
Has been admitted on stipulations

Arizona
Has been admitted on stipulations

Arkansas
Has been admitted on stipulations

California
Has been admitted on stipulations
New state law permits admissibility on stipulation, but not over objection

Colorado
Has not been admitted

Connecticut
Has not been admitted
*Once or more has been admitted over objection

Delaware
Has been admitted on stipulations

Florida
Has been admitted on stipulations

Georgia
> Has been admitted on stipulations

Hawaii
> Has not been admitted

Idaho
> *Has been admitted on stipulations
> *Once or more admitted over objection

Illinois
> Has not been admitted
> *Has been admitted on stipulations
> *Once or more admitted over objection

Indiana
> Has been admitted on stipulations

Iowa
> Has been admitted on stipulations

Kansas
> Has been admitted on stipulations

Kentucky
> Has been admitted on stipulations

Louisiana
> Once or more admitted over objection
> Admissible only in post-trial proceedings

Maine
> Has not been admitted

Maryland
> Has not been admitted

Massachusetts
> Once or more admitted over objection
>> Prosecution may introduce only to impeach, if defendant testifies. Defense may introduce only to corroborate his testimony, but over object and without prior agreement by the state

Michigan
> *Has been admitted on stipulations
> Once or more admitted over objection

Minnesota

Has not been admitted
*Has been admitted on stipulations
*Once or more admitted over objection
Trial court cases exist of stipulated admissibility and admissibility over objection

Mississippi
Has not been admitted

Missouri
Has been admitted on stipulations
Stipulated results limited to impeachment or corroboration of defendant's testimony

Montana
Has not been admitted

Nebraska
Has not been admitted

Nevada
Has been admitted on stipulations

New Hampshire
Has not been admitted

New Jersey
Has been admitted on stipulations

New Mexico
Once or more admitted over objection

New York
Has been admitted on stipulations
*Once or more admitted over objection

North Carolina
Has not been admitted
*Has been admitted over stipulations

North Dakota
Has not been admitted

Ohio
Has been admitted on stipulations

Oklahoma
Has not been admitted
*Once or more admitted over objection

Oregon
    Has not been admitted
    *Has been admitted on stipulations
    *Once or more admitted over objection

Pennsylvania
    Has not been admitted

Rhode Island
    *Has not been admitted

South Carolina
    Has not been admitted

South Dakota
    *Has been admitted on stipulations
    No positive appellate decision

Tennessee
    Has not been admitted

Texas
    Has not been admitted
    *Admitted over objection

Utah
    Admitted on stipulations

Vermont
    No positive appellate decision

Virginia
    Has been admitted on stipulations
        Use of polygraph evidence by civil service upheld on appeal to
        Circuit Court

Washington
    Has been admitted on stipulations

West Virginia
    Has not been admitted

Wisconsin
    Has not been admitted
    *Has been admitted on stipulations

Wyoming
    Has been admitted on stipulations

STATE LAWS ON THE POLYGRAPH

JURISDICTION

Alabama
A license is required
There are no limiting laws

Alaska
No license is required
There are some limiting laws
"Request or suggest"

Arizona
A license is required
There are no limiting laws

Arkansas
A license is required
There are no limiting laws

California
A license is required
There are some limiting laws
May not "demand or require". Attorney General of California ruled the law does not prevent an employer from "asking or requesting."

Colorado
No license required
There are no limiting laws

Connecticut
No license is required
There are some limiting laws

Delaware
No license is required
There are some limiting laws
Shall not "require, request or suggest"

Florida
A license is required

Georgia
A license is required
No limiting laws

Hawaii
No license is required
There are some limiting laws

Idaho
No license is required
There are some limiting laws

Illinois
A license is required
There are some limiting laws
Prohibits questions on religious, political, racial, sexual, or labor union matters. 1983 law prohibits requiring police officers to take a test

Indiana
A license is required
There are no limiting laws

Iowa
A license is required
There are some limiting laws

Kansas
A license is not required
There are no limiting laws

Kentucky
A license is required
There are no limiting laws

Louisiana
A certification is required
There are no limiting laws

Maine
A license is required
There are no limiting laws
For private polygraph practice, a private detective license is mandatory

Maryland

No license is required
There are some laws limiting use
    May not "require or demand"

Massachusetts
A license is required
There are some limiting laws
    License required for private practice. Law prohibits employer from "requiring or subjecting"

Michigan
A license is required
There are some limiting laws

Minnesota
A license is not required
There are some limiting laws
    "Request or require"

Mississippi
A license is required
There are no limiting laws

Missouri
No license is required
There are no limiting laws

Montana
A license is required
There are some limiting laws
    Shall not "require". Public law enforcement agencies are exempted

Nebraska
A license is required

Nevada
A license is required
There are no limiting laws

New Hampshire
No license is required
There are no limiting laws

New Jersey
No license is required
There are some limiting laws
    May not "influence, request or require". Pharmacists exempt, as are those who manufacture or distribute narcotics and

New Mexico
  A license is required
  There are no limiting laws

New York
  A license is not required
  There are no limiting laws

North Carolina
  A license is required
  There are no limiting laws

North Dakota
  A license is required
  There are no limiting laws

Ohio
  A license is not required
  There are no limiting laws

Oklahoma
  A license is required
  There are no limiting laws

Oregon
  A license is required
  There are some limited laws
    Shall not "require"

Pennsylvania
  No license required
  There are some limiting laws
    "Whoever requires"

Rhode Island
  No license is required
  There are some limiting laws
    "require or subject"

South Carolina
  A license is required
  No limiting laws

South Dakota
  A license is required
  There are no limiting laws

Tennessee
> A license is required
> There are no limiting laws

Utah
> A license is required
> There are no limiting laws

Vermont
> A license is required
> There are some limiting laws

Virginia
> A license is required
> There are some limiting laws
>> May not ask applicant or employee about sexual activities unless already convicted of a sex crime in Virginia

Washington
> A license is not required
> There are some limiting laws
>> "To directly or indirectly require"

West Virginia
> A license is required
> There are some limited laws

Wisconsin
> A license is not required
> There are some limiting laws
>> "Solicit, require or administer"

Wyoming
> A license is not required
> There are no limiting laws

District of Columbia
> No license is required
> There are some limiting laws
>> Shall not administer, accept or use the results. Metropolitan police, Fire Department and the Department of Corrections exempted of internal cases

Puerto Rico
> No license is required
> There are no limiting laws

NOTE: "Require or request" means a private company or agency may require the test to be there. "Suggest" is a real nebulous phrase meaning they can suggest you take a polygraph test, but you do not have to take the test. Want to bet you get the job if you don't take the test? The law says "may suggest, may not request or require."

Careful interpretation of these laws is required. You'd be surprised at the corporations who will require or suggest polygraph exams; 7-11's Southland Corporation is infamous for requiring these exams, where some multi-million job in the oil industry, for instance, may not require this. Yet a $4.00 an hour job in corporations such as 7-11 or sometimes fast food corporations require a test. They don't want you stealing their dollars or giving your friends free burgers.

The irony of this situation is little short of amazing.

AUDIO STRESS ANALYZERS

VOICE STRESS ANALYZERS: THE MIRACLE LIE DETECTOR?

In the last few years a new device has hit the market which makes some extravagant claims about being a stress analyzer and/or in some literature, a lie detector, which uses simply the human voice as the primary, and in this case, only factor determining result.

This device normally goes under the name PSE, Psychological Stress Analyzer, although it is sold by several companies now and may appear under other names such as Voice Analyzer or Voice Lie Detector. How well does it work? Well, for one thing, remember it's only measuring one particular aspect of the human body's autonomic nervous system. This is the micro-tremors in the voice. Granted there may be a relationship between these micro-tremors and stress, i.e., lies, but it is still only one feature. It does not have three or even five features to go on as many expensive lie detectors do.

However, it has a major advantage. It claims to work on recorded conversations, over the telephone, and can be used without the subject's knowledge. This means it is very easy to evade the state or federal test bans against lie detectors or laws regulating their use by using a PSE.

Let's take a look at the PSE and see exactly how it works and what can be done about it.

VOICE LIE DETECTORS

Voice analysis as a means of lie detection, or stress level measuring was introduced a few years ago by Dektor Counterintelligence and Security. They developed and market a device known as a Psychological Stress Evaluator. This consists of a device that analyzes the components of the voice spectrum and filters out the normal "speech", but saves minute FM changes imposed on these vocal "carriers". These FM changes are in the sub-audible band of 8 - 12 cycles and occur when the subject is in an UNSTRESSED condition, as stress increases these indiscernible modulations disappear. They are apparently caused by minute fluctuations in the muscles of the vocal chord and its surrounding mechanism.

The PSE is normally coupled to a tape recorder and a chart strip-recorder, in this fashion the presence or absence of these sub-audible indicators can be correlated with an exact word or phrase. To a practiced operator it is possible to pick out established stress patterns indicating a lie, a release of tension after the lie, and a return to the normal stress level on the next control or neutral question.

The detail of the recorded waveform allows the operator to make numerous judgments about the subject's reaction, or even his level of stress in any spoken phrase.

During this past year a new device known as Mark II has been introduced (invented by one Fred Fuller and developed by Technical Planning, Inc., and nationally distributed by Law Enforcement Associates). This device is also a voice analyzer, but it differs in several respects from the PSE; it measures an imposed modulation, or "tremolo" effect also, but goes for it in both the audible and sub-audible spectrum. The presence of this stress imposed effect is shown by adjusting the device for ambient noise and sensitivity and then depressing a button marked "analyze" after every answer or word to be analyzed is uttered. The numerical result is then shown to the operator directly be a LED (like they use in hand calculators) display. The operator compares the number to the numbers received by posing the neutral or control questions and a level of lie probability is established.

The Mark II can also be hooked up to a tape recorder and chart strip-recorder to provide a record of the test. It is sold in two models; one desk-top with LED display only, and one which comes in a carrying case with tape and chart recorders built-in.

On a polygraph the operator establishes a base line of stress and then assigns values to the various stress "spikes." A value of X is generally used to show a minor reaction to any one of the three indicators, a value of X1 is given to a stronger reaction and, as you might suspect X2 is assigned to a strong stress reaction.

If an X shows on at least two indicators, or an X2 shows on any one, it is usually considered to be a strong indication of a guilty reaction. Of course, these reactions should be compared with the control questions to get an accurate result.

In the PSE, the waveform is analyzed (Dektor has a training program for purchasers) for stress indicators and established stress reactions.

In the Mark II a numerical value must exceed that of a neutral or control question by a certain percentage to be considered suspect (this varies on the type of test between 20 and 30%).

How well do they work? Well, most of all of the polygraph operators claim the PSE and Mark II are invalid. This could be due, in part to a natural reaction called self-survival. Both Dektor and LEA furnish reports and testimonials that show their devices are at least as accurate as the polygraph, possibly more so.

Of course, it must be remembered that all three have to be evaluated by the operator. Some discrepancy may show up from operator to operator, especially in the polygraph and PSE. The Mark II is easier to use, and in fact, they claim most people can learn to utilize it correctly from their training manual and a couple of test tapes that they provide.

Another interesting facet of both the Mark II and PSE is that either can also operate from already recorded conversations, or over the phone, television or radio. Or they may be used "live" without the person realizing he is undergoing the test. Of course, in either of these situations the test is not really a test, and the controls are almost totally lacking, but a general level of stress can be established and additional stress points picked out.

Numerous people have used the PSE on Lee Harvey Oswald's various conversations and almost universally come out with the findings that there exists a lot of unexplained phenomena..... The Mark II people analyzed Patty Hearst's tape where she told of going over to the SLA on her own after the kidnapping. Their findings are a high stress level in general, but everything seems to be the truth. The only point of question is when she denies being "hypnotized", possibly indicating she did fear some sort of "brainwashing".

Personally I think either the Mark II or PSE have great potential in such unexplored areas as matrimony squabbles, poker games (especially the Mark II, just think what that would do to the art of bluffing), politics, used car salesmen, and just lots and lots of fun ideas.....

Of course, many are all ready in use by companies for employment verification, post-analysis of business meetings, checking on salesmen (even when they call in?), criminal investigations, and so on. You can bet your bottom dollar government agencies (CIA, FBI, or worse yet, maybe the IRS?) are checking these devices out, as well as a host of people want to use them for some personal gain.....

PSYCHOLOGICAL STRESS EVALUATOR, IS IT REALLY A "VOICE LIE DETECTOR?"

The prior report on the polygraph makes a number of salient points; the most obvious overriding conclusions that the machine does, indeed work.

However, it's a long way from perfect, and a bit too far from the exact to hang anyone on the results, which is why some states have made it illegal to use for any employment screening purposes.

It should also be noted that there is a possibility of misleading the machine with a bit of coached practice/or mechanical aids.

About 16 years ago a new "lie detector" appeared on the scene. This device was developed under contract for the Army. It indicated stress by measuring the amplitude variation in the low frequency FM component of human speech. This variation is caused by the same involuntary nervous system and endocrine changes that cause the reactions measured by "normal" lie detectors.

This device was/is hailed as a breakthrough because of several factors:

. it could be used without the subject's knowledge or consent.

. it could be operated on a live person or a tape recording of any conversation.

. it could be operated over the telephone

The flexibility of this system is obvious, any conversation that can be recorded can later be evaluated as conditions warrant.

The PSE was marketed by Dektor and LEA (who purchased the units from Dektor). Several other firms followed into this booming market with similar machines.

Many of the early machines used a meter or pen register to indicate degrees of stress and often gave certain levels that were to be positively read as lies... Now the trend seems to be to use colored (green for good, yellow for maybe and red for oh, oh...) LED's for indicators.

It also appears that many of the newer units have backed off the practice of showing certain readings to be "lies", substituting the term "stress indication..."

When the devices first came out *Penthouse* magazine had a writer borrow one and use it on his friends and the television program "To Tell the Truth". He was impressed with the results. Other such pseudo scientific tests followed. Most were favorably impressed with PSE.

Many manufacturers took to quoting these tests, or their own studies and advertising the units as "more accurate than a lie detector". Several police departments across the country have received permission to use the PSE (or its imitators) on subjects, numerous employers use them to screen applicants or help close business deals, and a number of licensed PSE operators are now open for business across the country much like the polygraph operators.

One firm even offers at-a-distance analysis. You tape your employee, wife, girlfriend, etc. and ship them the tape. By return mail they send you an analysis of who's telling what.....

The machines sell in the $2,000-$5,000 range and a number of PI's have purchased them to help with investigations. Some have not been pleased with the results.

Any lie detector or stress evaluation device is only as good as its operator. Furthermore any such device (as the polygraph study indicates) works better in some situations than in others. Is the PSE really "as accurate as the lie detector"?

I wanted to find the answer to two questions: Does the machine work with a good operator in a controlled situation? And if so, can a tape recorder actually reproduce the needed electronic information with a high enough accuracy as to be reliable seond-hand source?

The first study would have to utilize operators trained by the manufacturers to be a valid study. It would also have to be conducted in a scientific manner (not against a quiz show...) and with a large enough number of subjects to be valid.

I found two tests which met these criteria (as could be expected government intelligence agencies had a more than passing interest in a device which could separate the truth from the chaff, so to speak). The first test was conducted at Fordham University by a professor UNDER CONTRACT FOR THE U.S. ARMY LAND WARFARE LABORATORY. A nice touch as the unit was first conceived for this very outfit.

The second was a technical evaluation performed by the CIA. I am going to cover the pertinent parts of each of these tests, including a most, most interesting summary without adding, deleting, or shading any of the important parts of either test.

CIA STUDIES

CIA TECHNICAL EVALUATION

The central intelligence agency performed a series of studies on the PSE. The purpose of these tests was simply to evaluate the theory behind the instrument and if sound, ascertain if the function actually follows the theory.

Through a series of tests involving the machine's ability to process a secession of frequencies the CIA determined: the instrument is highly responsive to amplitude modulation (this is similar to AM radio, the amplitude, or strength of the signal imposed on a carrier determines its shape); the device is somewhat responsive to frequency modulation (can be compared to FM radio where the actual number of cycles, or frequency, is the deciding factor).

This was to be expected as the machine is designed to react to AM modulation on what is basically an FM signal - the human voice. However, they also concluded that AM modulation was SOMEWHAT interpreted by the PSE as a frequency modulation. The degree of interference was, however, small. Additionally they discovered high level input (source) material would actively distort the measurements.

Next a UHER 4000 recorder (this is a high level recorder used in film work. It is considerably higher in quality than one could expect to find a detective using, although not as good as a top end model such as a Nagra) was examined to see if the original signal was faithfully reproduced (in those frequency ranges which are PSE sensitive) to be used as a testing tool.

The results of this test were less than spectacular, the recorder did not reproduce the necessary frequencies with a high degree of reliability and in addition imposed its own signals on the tape which were "read" by the PSE as indications of stressful behavior in the subject.

One should note that the CIA report makes no real qualifying statements about the ability of the machine to detect lies and/or stress in a series of targets; it simply concludes that the machine does detect AM modulation in certain frequencies found in the human voice, but also reacts somewhat to the UNWANTED presence of FM modulation in those same sources.

On the other hand the report does raise serious doubts about the ability of a recorder to faithfully reproduce these small AM modulations without distortion or inducing completely false indications.

One has to ask one's self if a UHER recorder cannot live up to these qualifications. How can a cheaper model cassette (which runs at much slower speeds and produces must less fidelity) be expected to accomplish anything constructive? Also one must question the advertiser's claims that PSE like devices can operate "over the telephone" as the "fidelity" of a phone transmission which is limited to 500-3,000 Hz at best, and in effect dissolves and then recreates the human voice would seem to modify any results more than a recorder...

THE FORDHAM TESTS

CHAPTER 1. OBJECTIVES AND BACKGROUND

The present research had two objectives: to evaluate the capability of voice analysis as a lie detection technique and to compare the efficiency of two such devices with that of the polygraph. To achieve these objectives, the "simulated theft" paradigm, developed by the author in previous research, was adapted to the needs of the present experiment. Before beginning a description of this experiment, a brief review of the underlying rationale of lie detection procedures will be presented to provide a meaningful background for the proper evaluation of this research.

EMOTIONAL EXPRESSION

The basic characteristic of an emotional reaction is its widespread and diffuse aspect. All parts of the body are involved, internal as well as external. The hormonal responses to an emotional situation rapidly induce a variety of physiological perturbations among which blood pressure, respiration, and the psychogalvanic response have attained popularity as lie detection indices. While the use of these systems is sometimes identified with the specific area of lie detection, the physiological outputs are actually quite general, and have been accepted as valid expressions of an entire gamut of emotional responses. The particular problem in lie detection, which is not completely resolved, is the proper identification of the emotional components association with lying.

VOICE CHARACTERISTICS DURING DECEPTION

Voice-Emotion-Stress

Studies of, and training in, the vocal and temporal parameters of speech have always been considered the province of rhetoric and drama. This area has been rather neglected by psychologists whose research has focused more on personality and emotion as related to differences in vocal expression. Even here, results have been somewhat disappointing. Myers and Merluzzi (1971) report in a recent review that relationships between specific emotions and definite vocal patterns have neither been clear nor consistent. Recently, the development of voice spectrum analysis has opened up a new and intriguing technique for the study of these relationships, and the search for vocal characteristics that would have wide application still continues. At the present time, progress is being made in relating complex physical characteristics of speech to emotions and emotional stress. The primary problems are intersubject and intra subject variability; thus, using only physical characteristics of speech as a deter-mination of emotions or stress is still unreliable (Myers and Merluzzi, 1971, p.4.).

Much of the work in analyzing the speech spectrum in order to discriminate among emotional states has been initiated by Russian scientists. Some of the earliest research in spectrum analysis was developed in conjunction with the Russian space program, because of the expectation that this procedure would prove valuable in assessing degrees of stress in cosmonauts. The early interest of Russian scientists in the particularly intriguing problem of discriminating positive and negative emotions continues to the present (Popov et al., 1971).

Voice Analysis as a Lie Detection Technique

Myers and Merluzzi (1971) report only two studies in which judges attempted to detect lying solely by listening to the voices of speakers. In one report, the voices were presented over a public address system; in the other, they were on tape. In neither experiment was there a significant degree of correct identification of lying.

The electronic analysis of the speech spectrum might prove to be more diagnostic than ordinary signal acquisition and analysis by the human ear. Such electronic analysis is certainly more reliable and more objective, as it focuses exclusively on the physical characteristics of the sound. At the present time, two different instruments have been devised to explore this area, and though both make claims to measure "stress" or "psychological stress", their primary use seems to be directed at lie detection.

In the case of the Dektor Psychological Stress Evaluator, no experimental data have been made available. Publicity in the popular magazines, however, claims validity for the Dektor technique in criminal and non-criminal situations.

The second instrument, manufactured by Decision Control Incorporated, was "evaluated" by comparison with the polygraph in a study on three subjects. In a complex and lengthy report, Decision Control Incorporated, judged on issues they strongly approved or strongly disapproved. They were to maintain or create an impression of truth-telling in some situations; in others, they were to create an impression of lying. In the first two experiments, the subjects were viewed through a one-way mirror by observers who scored various aspects of the behavior, such as body position, movement in the body members, facial expressions, verbalizations and vocal activity. In the third experiment the subjects' behavior and speech were videotaped without their knowledge and later rated on the same behavioral characteristics. The results demonstrated that:

...When being deceitful communicators nodded and gestured less, exhibited less frequent leg and foot movements, assumed less immediate positions relative to their addresses, talked less, talked slower, had more speech errors and smiled more (Mehrabian, 1972, p. 103).

As previously indicated, experimental interest in this field is rather recent, while folklore and common experience have always acknowledged that concealed information must find an outlet in bodily expression. This "common-sense" knowledge has long been accepted during preliminary interviews with the subject is strongly advocated by Reid and Inbau (1966) in their text Truth and Deception. Various criteria by which to distinguish truth-telling from lying are also advocated. As an example:

A truth-telling person will not be upset by the suggestion of fingerprints, or footprint implications, whereas a liar will probably manifest considerable concern by such reactions as a delay in his answer, by looking away from the examiner, or by squirming around in the chair (1966, p. 14).

Whether he is aware of them or not, the polygraph operator will always be exposed to the nonverbal communications of the person he is interviewing or interrogating. The important issue is the determination of how much the nonverbal behavior is being utilized in the final decision process. If the polygraph operator is also the person who does the pre-test interviewing (and in most instances this is the case) how much of his final decision has already been determined before the polygraph examination has actually begun? It should be obvious that research in this area is urgently needed.

VOICE CHARACTERISTICS DURING DECEPTION

Voice-Emotion-Stress

Studies of, and training in, the vocal and temporal parameters of speech have always been considered the province of rhetoric and drama. This area has been rather neglected by psychologists whose research has focused more on personality and emotion as related to differences in vocal concluded: "The results of this study indicate that voice analysis provides results comparable to polygraph evaluations" (1971, p. 14). The nature of the report and the data presented make this conclusion difficult to verify; in any case the conclusion overshoots the data in that only three subjects were examined.

Before any such voice-spectrum instruments can expect to be accepted as valid, several requirements must be met by their manufacturers. Equipment developers must define more precisely what they mean by "stress", and must calibrate the physical output against known degree of stress. In addition, they must establish that the "stress" their machines measure is identified with whatever "stress" it is that permeates the lying response. Here again, a great deal of research remains to be done.

112

THE SIMULATED THEFT

Students were recruited as subjects by means of posted notices and by ads placed in the school newspaper. Once they indicated their willingness to participate in an "experiment", they were arbitrarily arranged in groups of three and given an appointment for the experiment. Because the subjects rarely arrived at exactly the same time, the Supervisor of the experiment was able to put one subject in one room and the other two in a separate room without the former seeing the latter. In almost all cases the three subjects did not know each other.

Once in the room the subjects were asked to fill out a form which requested census-type information. They were also asked to sign a pledge not to talk with anyone about this experiment for a period of a year. The census-type information enabled the Examiner to choose the appropriate questions for his interrogation.

The Supervisor then instructed the two individuals who were together as to the roles they were to assume. By drawing lots, one assumed the role of Thief, the other the role of Lookout. The Thief was to enter what he believed to be the unoccupied office of a female professor, open her handbag which was on the desk, examine the contents of the bag, and remove only the contents of the change-purse which was in the bag. The purse contained 21 dollars in bills wrapped around by a red ribbon.

The Thief's associate was to act as a Lookout, making sure that no one was around while the Thief entered and left the "professor's office". Since there were other offices nearby, and a students' activities room within 15 feet of the locus of the theft, the Lookout had an important and anxiety-provoking role in view of the uncertainties of students and professors whereabouts.

Although Thief and Lookout arrived near the professor's office together, they left the scene of the crime at different times so as not to attract attention or suspicion. Upon completion of his task, the Thief signalled the Lookout who immediately returned to the laboratory. In turn the Thief signalled the Lookout who immediately returned to the laboratory. The Thief left the scene of the crime, examined what he had taken from the purse, hid it on his person, and then returned to the laboratory. The two accomplices were instructed not to talk to each other after the theft was committed. As a result, the Lookout did not know what was stolen. While Thief and Lookout were waiting to be examined, the Supervisor made certain that no conversations were initiated between them.

Before being examined, the Innocent Suspect, who neither knew what happened nor who was involved, was given general instructions that there had "been a theft of some money in one of the faculty offices". He was advised that since he was not involved, he had no cause for worry. All that was required was that he answer the questions truthfully. (The Thief and the Lookout had already been instructed to deny all aspects of the theft, namely, the planning, participation, and execution).

Within each triad, subjects were examined in a random order.

THE EXAMINATION

Most of the examinations involved the use of a polygraph and a tape recorder with a lavaliere microphone. The subject was seated in front and to the side of the polygraph, which was thus placed to minimize its peripheral visibility to the subject during the testing. The Examiner was to the left and behind the apparatus while the Tape Monitor was more or less directly behind the subject. Both Examiner and Tape Monitor were unaware of the role each subject had played in the experiment.

The examination consisted of three parts: Interrogation with questionnaire, Modified Peak of Tension Test, and an Association Test. Each of these is described below.

QUESTIONNAIRE

After the pneumograph bellows, the lavaliere microphone, the PGR electrodes, and the blood-pressure cuff were attached, the subject was instructed to give a "Yes" or "No" answer to each of 30 questions included in the Questionnaire. To prevent excessive discomfort, the questionnaire was divided into four approximately equal parts, after each of which the pressure in the cuff was released and the subject given a brief rest.

Three types of questions were contained in the questionnaires: matter-of-fact questions, emotional standards and critical questions. As a designation suggests, the critical questions were directly related to the theft. There were four of them, each repeated once, thus providing a total of eight critical questions. The critical questions were:

> Were you an accomplice to the thief?
> Did you plan this robbery with someone else?
> Do you know who stole the money from Room 450?
> Do you have the stolen money with you?

Preceding each of these were emotional standard questions. These involved matters of a personal or family nature. In previous research they had been found to produce a moderate emotional reaction. These, too, were repeated; but no emotional standard preceded the same critical question more than once. Examples of these are:

> Do you have any brothers? sisters?
> Are you married? single?
> Have you served in the armed forces?
> Have you ever been arrested

Interspersed throughout the remainder of the questionnaire were the mater-of-fact or census-type questions, such as:

> Are you a Law student?
> Do you live in a one family house? an apartment?
> Do you own a motorcycle? car?
> Do you live in Brooklyn? Staten Island?

114

Of the matter-of-fact questions, only those which followed a critical question were so structured as to elicit a "No" response. All emotional standards also elicited a "No" response. The purpose was to guarantee a constant verbal evocation for these three questions. Only with this precaution could valid comparisons be made among ratios of emotional standards to critical, and among ratios of matter-of-fact to critical. In other words, every triad of questions, those preceding or following these triads, were answerable by "Yes." These "Yes" responses provided a change in response attitude and made the questioning seem quite natural to the subject.

PEAK OF TENSION TEST

Upon completion of the questionnaire, the Examiner instructed the subject to say "No" to each of the following numbers which represented dollars:

    15 17 19 21 23 25

As may be observed, the series is calculated to induce a build-up of tension toward the critical number 21, the amount stolen. Following the critical number, one would expect a decrease of tension, since the subsequent numbers are irrelevant to the Thief. As for the Lookout and Innocent Suspect, no such regular rise and fall of tension was expected, since neither knew what amount had been stolen.

ASSOCIATION TEST

The final test procedure included two lists of words used as association tests. These lists follows:

)1 APPLE EAGLE HANDBAG PENCIL TABLE LOOKOUT ROADSIDE
)2 WINDOW WARLIKE RIBBON SPRINGTIME OCEAN

The underlined words have direct reference to the theft. Those in the first list involve the Thief and the Lookout. The word RIBBON in the second list could have meaning only to the Thief.

The Peak of Tension and Association procedures comprised approximately 40 percent of testing time. They were used to provide additional criteria for the differentiation of the Thief and Lookout, a matter to which the questionnaire devoted only 25 percent of testing time (two of eight critical questions).

POST EXAMINATION AND DEBRIEFING

When the three test procedures had been completed, the Examiner instructed the subject to return to the Supervisor. After the last subject of a triad was examined, the Examiner and Tape Monitor, each working independently, recorded their impression as to who was the Thief, who the Lookout, and who the Innocent Suspect. This procedure provided a basis for evaluating the ability of the Tape Monitor to size up suspects merely on the basis of their behavior and voice characteristics. The Examiner

115

potentially had an additional source of information -- the polygraph record. However, as mentioned earlier, the Examiners felt that, in view of the continuing attention to mechanical details, position of next question to be asked, etc., very little immediate record interpretation was possible. As a result they considered their impression of the person's behavior before, during, and immediately after the examination to be significant factors in their identification of the role each subject assumed in the experiment. Contrast between the success ratios of Tape Monitors and Examiners in these immediate global judgments if found, might suggest in fact, that the Examiners had made some use of the chart information available to them.

Meanwhile the subject who completed the examination was being debriefed by the Supervisor. He was also asked to rate his emotional reactions during each phase of the theft (Thief and Lookout) and during the interrogation itself (all members of triad).

One month following the completion of the experiment, all subjects were contacted for the drawing of prizes. This fulfilled the promise made during recruitment and during the initial instructions by the Supervisor.

Contacts with subjects tended to confirm the belief that no subject talked about the experiment before it was completed. Cooperation of subjects seemed particularly good in this matter.

PHYSICAL FACILITIES AND INSTRUMENTATION

PHYSICAL FACILITIES

The experimental facilities included a suite of three adjacent rooms, one of which was used for interrogating the subjects. The other two rooms were used to accommodate the subjects before and after the examination period. They were furnished with tables and chairs, and served as waiting and instruction rooms. The examining room contained the polygraph and recording instruments.

The room from which the money was stolen was one floor above, and at the opposite end of the corridor. Prior to its use for this project, it had been a testing room, though no different from others which were being used as offices by faculty. It was arranged to look like a faculty office, with books and reading material spread about on the desk. With the handbag on the desk, it appeared that the faculty member had just stepped out for a moment.

INSTRUMENTATION

Two traditional field polygraphs (Stoelting) were available for use throughout the experiment. The one which provided the basic data was a compact Md I Executive. A Stoelting Deceptograph which was used for training the Examiners was always on hand for backup purposes.

A high quality recorder, Uher 4000 Report L, was used to record the interrogation sessions. Tape speed was 7-1/2 inches per second. A lavaliere microphone was also used. In the early phase of the experiment, the microphone was generally placed on the table next to the subject. During the latter part it was uniformly placed over the neck of the subject and rested comfortably on his chest.

A model of the Voice Stress Analyzer was used in the evaluation of the voice records. The instrument, produced by Decision Control Inc., extracts speech energies in two frequency bands, 100 to 120 hertz, and 500 to 800 hertz; and forms the ratio of the corresponding energies. This ratio is assumed to change with variation in stress. The instrument presents a visual record on paper tape of energy ratios extracted from a given speech signal. In the present research the speech signal was the word "No". The peak amplitude of the energy ratio is the value used to assess the degree of stress, and thus the degree of involvement in the simulated theft.

The Dektor Psychological Stress Evaluator was also used to analyze the same tape recordings obtained in the simulated theft. A brief account of its use has been provided by George F. Cake Co. in a page of advertising copy. An excerpt from this description follows:

> It makes use of specific voice qualities which reflect visually or aurally undetectable changes resulting from small changes in the degree of psychological stress... Either "yes" or "no" answers, narrative answers, or conversational utterances may be used to accomplish the evaluation...the voice frequencies employed are well with the 300 to 3,000 hertz frequency band.

There are several levels or modes of analysis, and the first of these is analogous to that obtained with the Voice Stress Analyzer. Additional modes involve a sophisticated visual evaluation of frequency patterns. Expertise in these procedures required extensive training. In this present experiment all analyses performed on the Psychological Stress Evaluator were done by an expert who had been trained at Dektor.

SUBJECTS

All subjects were students at Fordham University. The majority ranged from 18 to 25 years of age; only three were younger than 18 and eight older than 25. The sample included 116 men and 58 women.

There were 57 complete triads. Of these 45 involved both the polygraph and tape recorder; 12 triads used the tape recorder alone during the interrogation. An additional classification of the triads showed that 18 were female in composition, 36 were male, and 3 were mixed. Of these 2 of the female, 7 of the male, and the 3 mixed triads were interrogated by the non-polygraph procedure.

As expected, a number of difficulties arose during the execution of the experiment. In triad 5, one subject confessed. Triad 39 was eliminated because of a strong suspicion that the subjects had previous knowledge of the details of the experiment. Triad 40 was also discarded because of non-responsiveness, possibly due to mechanical difficulties. Several other triads contained poor records in one or another component.

These records were not discarded whenever two of the other components generated adequate tracings.

EXAMINERS AND RATERS

Four Examiners were used. During the course of each simulated theft, one of the Examiners served as polygraph operator while another assumed the role of Supervisor for that experimental triad. Usually these roles were reversed when several triads were available.

All four Examiners had graduate degrees -- two had PhD's and two, M.A. degrees. Two were male and two were female. All were psychologists with a strong background in the physiological bases of emotional responsiveness. Before beginning the experiment, they were given a short course in polygraph operation by an acknowledge expert in the field from another institution.

After completing the interrogation of an experimental triad, the Examiner filed the polygraph charts for a period of approximately two weeks, to allow specific memories of any session to fade before he started his formal analysis of the records. He rated the polygraph responses from all three components of the interrogations and then gave his decision as to the role of each member of the triad. This was done for each triad separately. For ready reference, this rating procedure will be called "Triad Analysis". This is to be contrasted with "Individual Analysis" wherein each individual record, isolated from its triad, is judged on its own merits. In the Triad Analysis, the rater has all three records of a triad for comparison, and should he be correct in two of the judgments, he would necessarily be correct in his judgment of the third record even though he never looked at it. In the individual analysis, the rater made his judgment of subject involvement. (Thief, or Lookout, or Innocent Suspect) only on the basis of the tracings in that record alone. There were no clues from the previous or subsequent record since these belonged to different triads.

While Triad Analysis was done by the four Examiners, the Individual Analysis of polygraph records was reversed for two other experienced polygraph operators. With these data, then, both types of comparison were made: accuracy of polygraph and voice ratings under Individual Analysis; and accuracy of polygraph and voice ratings under Triad Analysis.

RESULTS

Despite the complexity of the procedures and analyses, the results can be readily classified into several interrelated categories. The first section will deal with the polygraph results: the accuracy of judgment in Examiner and rater, and the detectability of lying in male and female subjects. In a sense this introductory evaluation has to do with the validity of the experimental procedure. If the polygraph operator could not detect emotional variation in the responses of different role-playing subjects, there would be some doubt as to the adequacy of the polygraph as a criterion against which to test the validity of the voice analyzers as lie detection devices.

The second section will analyze the immediate global judgments of Examiners and Tape Monitors. These results should provide evidence as to whether behavior is a nonverbal communicator of the internal attitudes and feelings of the suspect and whether ordinary people can decode these messages with better than chance accuracy. The results provided in this section can also be used to validate the experimental procedure in that they may provide evidence that the experimental procedure does in fact induce specific behaviors in the suspect which reflect his guilty or innocent frame of mind.

In the third section the evaluation of the Psychological Stress Evaluator as a lie detector will be done under both analytic modes--Individual and Triad Analysis. Further, the accuracy of the Psychological Stress Evaluator will be determined when used with the polygraph and when used alone. This comparison should indicate whether the stress induced by the polygraph attachments affects the adequacy of the voice records for lie detection purposes.

The final section will present the statistical analysis of the peak responses of the Voice Stress Analyzer (VSA) to the critical questions during the interrogation. Since no specific criteria for detecting deception have been provided by the VSA research manual, the procedure adopted was to make an analysis of the VSA responses for each of the eight critical questions, taken separately for each triad. Within each triad, the responses were ranked for each of the questions. The sum of the ranks for each experimental role (Thief, Lookout, Innocent Suspect) could thus be used to indicate whether there was differential voice responsiveness among subjects assuming each of the three roles.

SUMMARY

This experiment used 174 subjects in a simulated theft scenario to establish the accuracy of voice analysis as a means of lie detection.

Along with the voice analyzers a polygraph was utilized under the same circumstances. Both devices were operated by trained operators and the experiment was observed by monitors.

--The polygraph achieved an accuracy of 76%.

--Independent polygraph raters, who knew nothing of the experiment, viewed the results at a later date with an accuracy of 50-60%.

--The voice stress analyzers varied between 19-44%. AS THE GROUPS WERE TRIADS PURE CHANCE IS 33%!

--The tape monitors and examiners outscored the voice analysis people by nearly double SIMPLY BY OBSERVATION OF THE SUBJECTS!

In the words of the report, "The failure of the voice-analysis techniques to detect these differences cannot, then, be attributed to insufficient emotionalism in the subjects. Rather it would seem to be a matter of insensitivity or other inadequacy in the devices themselves in the present state of development."

Note: Parts of the above reprinted by permission of Lee Lapin.

ONE EXAMINER'S EXPERIENCES WITH A STRESS ANALYZER

The first pertinent fact in this little sidebar is: of all the major PSE and stress analyzer dealers that I approached (Dektor, Mason, Security Research International, etc.) only ONE would even consider letting me test one of their units.....

All the others were quite the pinnacle of friendliness until they realized I wanted that specific piece of gear. Mr. X suddenly became involved in a perpetual conference and I was told "we can't let you try out a stress analyzer."

Only VIKING INTERNATIONAL loaned me a stress detector and said, "Do what you want, then print the results."

The device I tested was VIKING Stress Analyzer (made elsewhere) selling for $2300. This price includes a very nice leather, Samsonite briefcase, the unit itself, a nice tape recorder, a telephone loop induction device, patch cords, instructions and a demonstration/test tape. I should point out that at $2300 this is one of the cheapest units on the market, even though they all work pretty much the same.

I spent some time getting to know the machine; first, I ran the test tape through to make certain the device was functioning as it should. Then I ran the demonstration tape through the device. The unit has three green, three yellow and three red LEDS. The green indicates the presence of micro-tremors in the voice range (or lack of stress), the yellow indicates few micro-tremors and the red mean oh-oh. The unit also has a threshold control that needs to be reset for different ambient voice noise levels.

I used the unit on friends, strangers, tapes and the telephone. Several interesting factors did emerge. Now please understand this is NOT a scientific test, but it is meant to duplicate what the average buyer might experience:

1. The device does work, sort of. There are few definite "lies". Most statements are a mix with several different LEDS showing.

2. Learning to ask the right questions in the right manner is the key to any success and this is NOT easy.

3. A simple instruction book IS NOT ENOUGH TRAINING. Several companies including Dektor offer a 4 day to 2 week training program. You really should consider paying for one of these programs if you are going to lay out the money for a stress analyzer.

4. Some people do not react in the same fashion as the "norm". To be specific, I tested the unit out on several friends who are professional announcers for one of the networks. The fact that they have spent 15 years learning to modulate their voices to sound steady DID make them much tougher subjects than the average person.

5. At best, the device is a tool, and basing lifelong decisions on its results would be a bit shaky.

6. On the other hand, I am no longer seeing a girlfriend due to the results of this device, so there is some validity, ESPECIALLY if you understand how to use interrogation techniques to separate the wheat from the chaff.

My other major complaint with stress analyzers is their price. At $2300, you can buy a VIKING and still spend $1800 on a user's course without paying any more than many companies ask for the device alone. It is not a complicated device to build. Two companies have offered cheap units (Omnitronics and Edmund), which sold for under $200! Neither company is selling the units anymore because the mass price meant it sold to too many housewives who had no idea how to use such a device and then complained about it.

But the point is that the units worked about the same as the $4000 specials for a lot less money and someone else could sell them again for this price making the whole idea a more viable concept.

HOW TO BEAT ANY STRESS ANALYZER

Unlike the lie detector (polygraph) there is a very simple way to invalidate any PSE or stress analyzer test: Drop your voice down to a fairly low register and say the stall-syllable, "ahhhh", as if someone has just asked you if you have ever cheated on your wife... "ahhhhhh, well, ahhhhhh, noooo.....not exactly."

The "ahhhh" is a non-modulated tone. IT WILL LIGHT UP THE RED LEDS like a Christmas tree. Try speaking in that same manner - a low, steady raspy growl from the back of your throat.

The machine will now indicate everything you say as a lie.

OTHER METHODS

One problem with the above technique is that it is pretty obvious you are doing it.

Another approach is to read your answers from a paper, speaking in a monotone as much as possible. This is not foolproof, works best over the phone where the person cannot see you do it, and you must have all the answers written down to any side of a possible question.

Do you notice how many politicians do this?

Another shot is drugs. I did test two subjects in the clear and under Valium (a preparation of Diazepam marketed by Roche). The Valium DID induce a calming effect that further blurred the results and did cause several lies to pass with only green or two greens and one or two yellows.

Booze also muddies the test somewhat, but not to the same degree as Valium, and is easier to detect.

Next time you talk to an insurance adjuster over the phone and he wants to record your call, you might want to remember these tips.

PSE COUNTERMEASURES, ACTIVE

Rather than pad this book by going through test by test or case history basis, let us just add that all of the chemical and mechanical measures encountered and tested in response to the polygraph deception section, seem to work as well or better on any kind of voice stress analyzer.

If we stop and consider for a second, this is a natural phenomena as the PSE or any other voice stress analyzation device uses only one indicator of stress. That is, micro-tremors in the voice, which is a portion of the autonomic nervous system as are the three to five modes measured by the normal polygraph machine. Therefore, any chemical or mechanical or practice indicator that will work on the polygraph seems to work even better on a PSE. Add to this the fact the voice stress analyzation is a new science, if indeed it is a science, and the fact that the machines operate with a number of different subjective phenomena including recording technique, closeness to subject, over the telephone, etc., and one will find the mechanical, chemical and active/passive measures tend to work better on the PSE than they do on the lie detector.

The problem herein is denoting when the PSE is in use since it is in theory impossible to tell if a PSE is being used on a subject, since it can be used from a tape recording or over the phone, Our attitude is it is better to be safe than sorry. If you are making a report to a job interview where you feel a PSE may be used, especially in states where it's illegal to record someone's conversation without their consent, therefore, the persons using the PSE recording act are committing a felony or if you are talking over the phone to an insurance investigator, police department or other similar type of agency, it may be wise to employ any of these mechanical active/passive methods at hand to help defeat the PSE.

HANDWRITING ANALYSIS

GRAPH ANALYSIS

HANDWRITING TELLS ALL

Graph analysis is becoming an extremely popular field and is being employed by more and more companies to give an idea of the inherent characteristics of job applicants and people considered for promotion. Most graph analysts claim it is impossible to hide or disguise one's handwriting to change the overall look or basis of one's personality because of the level of concentration required to sustain this falsification is immense and will show through.

However, if one concentrates strictly on the areas of handwriting that are used as deception indicators, in other words the things that are looked at by graph analysts hired by employers to read job applications, etc., to indicate whether the applicant is trustworthy or dishonest, one can successfully avoid these indicators in one's handwriting and at least pass the honesty part of the test, which is what this book is all about.

One of the first things most analysis analysts look at is a full page sample or block of your handwriting to see how organized you are, how evenly spaced the lettering is, if the lines are also equally spaced, and an important factor they look for is how much pressure you use on the pen itself during the sample. This is the reason many employers now will not allow the use of a felt tip pen as it is much, much easier to read the pressure application on a ballpoint pen.

Unless they tell you that it isn't allowed, a wise move is to use a felt tip pen so your pressure cannot be used as an indication by a graph analyst. A heavy pressure normally indicates someone who is stubborn, or very definitive or very insistent on getting his own way. While too light of a pressure can indicate someone who is insecure, wishy washy or a short attention span. Medium, average pressure that doesn't dent the paper too hard, is what a graph analyst will look for as an indicator of a normal personality.

One way to establish your pressure is simply to compare an average sample of your handwriting with several of your friends or other people. Look at the back of the page and it will become apparent immediately how much pressure each of you has applied.

A person who writes with extremely heavy pressure, pressure that dents the paper, is a person who is very likely to react heavily to stress. This fact can be used in the job determination itself or can be used in furthering a kinesic interview situation by knowing this person is going to be stress affected.

The slant to the handwriting is also considered in with pressure. They actually can measure it on a meter. If the slant is towards the right at much less than a 45 degree angle and fairly consistent, this tends to mean a logical person, a person who prizes thinking over emotions and a fairly stable person. You should note that it doesn't make any difference on this whether a person is right handed or left handed.

Even more forward towards the right indicates he is more emotional and extreme right hand leaning (see the sample) indicates emotional instability.

emotional instability

An extrovert's handwriting will slant quite a bit to the right while an introvert's may have a backward slant. This could indicate emotionally withdrawn people, people who are guarding themselves from something, people who have something to hide. (Again, see the sample)

something to hide

If it goes back and forth between these two extremes and is quite scribbly looking (see the sample), this indicates irresponsibility and inability to make a decision.

inconsistent thought process

INSIDE LOOPS

Notice how an O has an inside loop in it at the top to the right. This indicates secrecy. If the loop is to the left at the top, it indicates actual deception. Now this could be self-deception or it could be lying or cheating. If there are double loops in the O, it indicates a person is deliberately holding back information. This characteristic is often found in the handwriting of doctors because as one might suspect, doctors often hold back certain facets of information from their patients.

double loops

Note the large loop in a K called a buckle. This implies defiance or stubbornness. Also note the double loops which indicate deceit.

The following sample denotes aggression.

strange book

Note the sample below with the hooks and double loops. This indicates deception or the person is in fact, lying.

hooks and loops

Look at your handwriting and see if it includes any of this and endeavor to eliminate it if it does, at least on job applications or anything having to do with truth interviewing situations.

One particular handwriting move is not going to definitely indicate anything, but as in kinesic interviewing, a group of them or a cluster of hooks, loops, etc. will prove to a graph analyst you are deceptive or lying. For instance, double loops mean deceitful and hooks combined means ambition. So here you have someone who could very likely steal or lie.

SINCERITY

all this is true

Note in this sample there are no double loops, all the I's are dotted with a round little circle, instead of just dotting it. This indicates sincerity and might be a good habit to cultivate.

NEAT VERSUS SLOPPY

The neatness of a person's handwriting does not necessarily indicate this trait carries through in their life style. A person who writes very neatly is generally thought to think slower than he writes. He thought everything through before he put it on paper. Whereas a person who writes quickly or sloppily, is thinking faster than he is writing. His thoughts are going rapidly and the writing is almost secondary in an attempt to catch up and record what he's thinking. (see the sample)

This does not hold true when we're speaking of a person's signature. A scrawled signature implies the person does not want himself to be known. He is hiding himself. It does not necessarily indicate deception but it indicates a person who does not want his innermost thoughts to be known. He may be a little more private inside.

On the other hand, a person who writes very carefully, his signature that is, or even prints it, is someone who wants people to know for sure, for certain what he is saying. He wants to leave no doubt about himself, his statement and his personality.

People who have a real flashy signature or underline it or have some particular decoration on it, have a high opinion of themselves. (see the sample)

GENERAL QUALIFICATIONS

If you are applying for a specific job, there is a chance a graph analyst will look at your handwriting to see how your traits would fit the job. If its a job where you have to be organized, a detail kind of person, you'd want your handwriting to be fairly detailed, your I's dotted, things even and symmetrical.

On the other hand, if it's a job of a creative nature, they are much less likely to be impressed with the symmetry and slowness of the writing as they would be with a more creative writing style.

One can adapt his writing to a specific job, but this is not entirely the purpose of this book. If you are interested there are a number of good books on the subject. We suggest you purchase one and study it.

DRUG TESTING

DRUG SCREENING PROCEDURES

The idea of periodic or spot drug screening is increasing in popularity at an alarming rate. The prodcedures involved, besides violating one's sense of privacy and propriety are subject to enough of a degree of inaccuracy to indicate the unsafeness of basing a job or a law suit upon their findings.

Some testing facilities and test marketing firms have admitted only a 98% accuracy rate; hence 2 empoylees out of every hundred tested may be marked positive EVEN THOUGH THEY WERE, IN FACT, NEGATIVE!

Employers may simply decide to include a program of drug testing due to the dangerous or confidential work employees are doing, or such procedures may in fact by instituted due to a prejudice on the employer's part or due to the "work" or an "undercover agent".

The latter may be a paid professional or simply another empoyee with an axe to grind.

Often these informants may be blackmailed or coerced by threats to the job situation itself. The most common type of drug testing is urine testing. It should be noted this process is actually a two step test. The specimens must be collected and then identified and then analyzed. Depending on whose doing the collecting many times less of an import is placed on the first part of the testing. Often if someone has reason to think that they are going to show positive in a drug test, this is where the test is "beaten." A number of variables come into play which can work either for or against the person being subjected to the test.

Who are the people who are making the test? Are they doctors, nurses, laboratory employees or are they simply employees of the firm asking for the tests? Is the process handled by people who are fully trained and understand the legal requirements to establish what is known as a chain of custody. A number of lawsuits have upheld the concept that if any carelessness or evidence of error can be proven to exist in the collection and storage of urine to be tested it becomes impossible to substantiate any positive test results. This type of lawsuit has benefited a number of persons who were discharged or otherwise punished for a positive finding in their screening.

In one instance simply the cooperation of another employee who testified to the lack of security during the specimen collection procedure was enough for the court to throw out the test results and find in favor of the defendant. It is generally held that people who are not specifically trained to collect urine samples will not normally exercise the caution required to establish an accurate or legal claim. Obviously a number of such errors are induced by persons who fear their test will come out positive and as such are not happenstance. This loophole in the testing procedure is exploited by both testees and attorneys at a later stage.

Simply because a person is a health professional, i.e., a nurse or a technician does not in a legal sense establish they are competent to conduct a drug screening procedure. If an employer does not go to the expense and trouble of using a health professional for the first step, that is the collection stage, but rather elects to use his own employees, it is much easier to establish the possibility of error or doubt in any drug test. Of course, some employers will have the foresight to have their employees involved in the test trained and/or certified by a professional screening agency.

There are a few laboratories and a fewer number of security agencies who offer trained collection technicians as of this writing. It is extremely probably that this lucrative field will broaden over the next few years.

Due to the relative ease in substitution or alteration of samples, many employers have taken measures such as unannounced, on the spot checking and/or the use of undercover or loyal employees to point out problem areas as well as add their testimony to the drug testing results. The accuracy of any non-professional forced testing procedure must be questioned.

Besides the legal responsibility of the employer or testing agency to prove correct and valid collection procedures, they must be also able to prove a continuing sequence of security and sample identification. This includes cold storage for any sample until the actual testing or confirmation is performed as well as the ability to prove physical protection of the samples up to and including anti-burglar systems and high security locks at the laboratory or place of testing. It is not unheard of for collection technician or laboratory personnel to substitute samples willingly or to avoid any implication of carelessness or wrongdoing on their part should samples become mislaid or spoiled.

Very few collection agencies or services offer the level of security necessary to establish a legal chain of custody. The slack in this end of the business benefits no one, least of all the target of the screening.

While it is possible to encounter blood testing, this normally requires consent and is prohibitively expensive. Nearly all the drug screening now is based on the testing of a urine sample.

A common misconception is that drug testing or screening procedures actually test for the presence of a drug in the subject's body. In reality the tests search for a reaction to one of a number of chemicals produced after a person's body ingests a drug. Because of this it is possible to produce a positive result long after the actual use of any drug. The window for a reliable test varies greatly with such factors as the drug family involved, the amount ingested, the person's weight and rate of metabolism. It is impossible to say with any degree of accuracy the exact length of time any drug may be detected. As a rule of thumb cocaine is usually detectable 48 hours after use while any marijuana based substance can usually be spotted for several weeks after indulgence.

No drug testing procedure can actually indicate impairment, intoxication or abuse. Rather it will simply indicate the possibility, or if you will, probability, of some use sometime in the past.

There are several varieties of testing procedures used in urinalysis. However, most have in common two stages of operation: the first stage is known as screening and is performed simply to mark specimens that appear to have a positive reaction to at least one type of drug. This preliminary screening test is normally not as accurate or reliable as the confirmation phase which follows. In any testing scenario the two stages should be performed by different methods of at least the same or better reliability. If the confirmation stage is not different and at least as reliable, it is normally discarded in any legal situation.

All drug screening methods have in common the standard practice to screen for eight different classes of drugs. These classes include amphetamines, barbiturates, benzodiazepines such as Valium, cannabinoids, cocaine, Methaqualone, opiates and phencyclidine or PCP. Each separate type of drug requires separate and different screening procedure.

Before we examine the actual types of tests, it is necessary to grasp the idea that the terms positive/negative, or in this case guilty/innocent are at best arbitrary in every test. The manufacturers of all drug testing equipment and reagents include a cutoff level below which findings are considered negative and above which they are considered positive. This cutoff level is not standard and may vary by as much as 100% between different manufacturers. In some cases the testing company or the employer of said company may establish a different cutoff level than the manufacturer recommends in order to avoid the possibility of uncertainty and error inherent in these testing procedures.

Cutoff level is normally expressed in nanograms per milliliter abbreviated ng/ml. A nanogram is one-billionth of a gram and one ng/ml is one part per billion. Cutoff levels normally are established in the range of 50 ng/ml to 100 ng/ml. This variance in cutoff levels adds to the confusion and uncertainty of any drug test.

Drug Screening Methods

Most common method of the drug screening segment for the urinalysis is Thin-Layer Chromatography or TLC. In this test a single drop of treated urine is placed on a glass plate and dye is induced. The urine will react to the dye undergoing colored and physical changes with a relationship to any drug by-products involved. Unfortunately this test must be interpreted by the person performing it. TLC is the least sensitive among all the drug testing methods. However, it is also the least expensive and therefore the most common. The color pattern that is interpreted by the screener is temporary and fades quickly leaving no permanent record.

Enzyme Immunoassay or EIA is the second most commonly utilized screening procedure. In EIA a reagent is added to a urine sample. If any drug byproduct is present antibodies will attach themselves to it causing a color reaction. In this test a spectrophotometer is used to measure the severity of the reaction providing a more accurate reading than the TLC. Although this test is more sensitive than the TLC, it is less sensitive than gas chromatography and much less sensitive than gas chromatography/mass spectrometry combined. However, it can be performed with portable equipment outside of a laboratory. It does not require an excessive amount of technical knowledge to operate the equipment but by the same token is subject is to a greater risk of contamination or inaccuracy due to human error. The EIA is more costly than the TLC.

Radioimmunoassay or RIA is the third and most accurate type of screening procedure. In RIA a reagent that has been designed to react to a specific drug class has been added to the urine sample. Again antibodies will attach themselves to any drug byproduct present. Then the solution is exposed to a material that is radioactive and a gamma radiation counter is utilized to measure the radiation emitting from the sample. This produces a radiation pattern that can be compared to known samples to establish a positive drug reaction. This test is approximately the same in sensitivity as the EIA. It is fairly well established although it does require trained technician and a licensed facility due to the materials utilized.

It is during the collection or during one of the above screening methods where the possibility for error or substitution exists. One method that has been successfully employed in TLC screening and has had limited success in the other methods is described here.

URINALYSIS

Even though a I write this, congress has pretty much outlawed mandatory polygraph testing for federal employees and many states have outlawed it in the private sector as well. Because of the unproven accuracy of the unit, and the discretion left open to the tester himself, more and more agencies are allowing or even requiring drug screening tests.

This is as large an invasion of privacy as the polygraph test, if not a larger one. In many cases, the testing is no more accurate than the polygraph test. Let me qualify this by saying if a blood test it taken to a hospital and actually run through a high-quality analysis for the by-products of certain drugs, it can be fairly well proven these drugs have been ingested. Contrary to popular belief, drugs do not stay in one's bloodstream for 30 days after you've smoked marijuana for instance. However, the by-products of smoking marijuana or taking cocaine or other drugs, do tend to remain in the bloodstream for some time.

Unfortunately, this type of testing is very expensive and complicated and is not practical to do on a large scale basis. The tests that are available are usually chemical reaction tests that simply test the urine for the presence of certain drugs. The problem with this is these tests are notoriously inaccurate and may be up to 30% inaccurate on their own

This means they may give a guilty response when there is no drug present in the sample. This is not good and causes people to lose their jobs for no reason and brings about various other problems. The urinalysis test will often react to other things besides the drug they are looking for in a positive manner. This also invalidates the test.

One way to take care of most urinalysis tests on the market as I write this is to add two to three teaspoonsful of salt to your urine sample. This will change the PH and salinity of the sample to make it outside the range the test is able to test for. These tests test in a fairly limited PH and salinity range and do not have the capabilities, since they are simple chemical reaction test, to test anything that is outside the range. Once you pass this salinity level, the test will read negative. You will pass the test no matter what sample is in your blood. There are no written urinalysis test on the market now. It might be convenient to pick up a little salt package from a restaurant and carry it with you if you have any reason to suspect you might come under this type.

After the screening portion of the test is completed, samples of the negative reaction or reaction below the established cutoff point are discarded. Any sample that tests positive is normally subjected to a further test known as the confirmation test.

Confirmation methods are normally based on Gas Chromatography or GC. In order to produce a positive confirmation of the earlier screening reaction, GC separates chemical compounds on a column of absorbent material. In preparation for this separation the urine sample is vaporized by heating it and the results are compared to known patterns.

GC is more sensitive than any of the above screening methods and offers some attempt at determining the quantity of drug byproduct present in the sample. This test requires quite involved equipment and highly skilled operators. It is generally not possible to conduct a GC test with anyone except trained laboratory or hospital personnel.

It is apparent on observation that any drug test is somewhat arbitrary, dependent on a number of variables and is open to purposeful influence at one or more stages. If one is the subject of a drug screening test or conversely, if one is evaluating a laboratory or other facility for conducting a drug test, a number of questions must be answered: what type of screening and confirmation procedures are utilized; is Thin-Layer Chromatography avoided; are the technician or employees specifically trained in all avenues of testing techniques; can the facility provide expert witnesses to testify; is an acknowledgment of the drug abuse policy in question obtained from the targets as well as a consent to the test and information regarding prescription drugs that may interfere with any testing procedure on file; is the chain of custody performed to legal standards including safeguards for the specimens, the results and the confidentiality of the persons taking the test; is the storage facility for positive samples adequately protected from inside or outside contamination, substitution or switching of specimens?

It is also necessary to ascertain the type of drug classes the facility routinely tests for as well as the number of tests actually performed. The latter figure is important as a necessary volume of tests, normally 300 per week, is necessary to establish knowledge of procedures and ability. Any evidence that the facility does not meet these standards or that they are not certified for drug testing, automatically induces doubt to any findings.

As the use of drug screening as a prerequisite for employment and promotion increases so will the legal battles concerning the safeguards of the persons being tested.

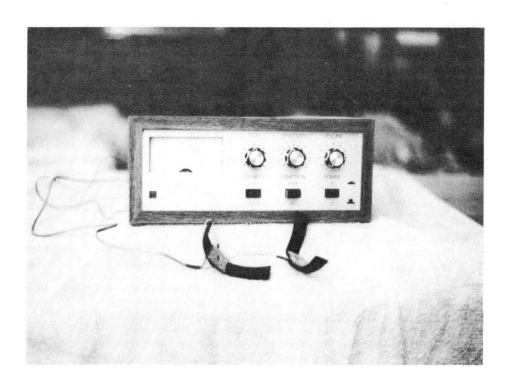

The GSR.

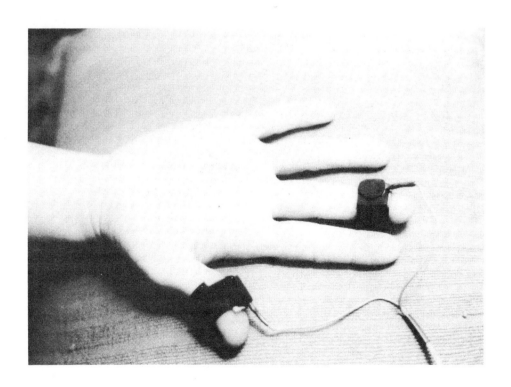

GSR electrodes.

Baseline.

Overly friendly.

Subject is mirroring the interviewer.

Correct distancing for kinesic situation.

An example of attacking the middle zone.

Interviewer "opening" to relieve tension.

"Bundling up" in a chair.

"Studious" subject; maybe be in conrtol of the situation.

Exaggerated "NO!"

Covering mouth.

Looking away.

Listening intently.

Head tilt; listening.

Profiling.

Looking at fingernail.

Pleading.

145

3 Whites.

Breaking eye contact.

Nose contact.

Hiding eyes.

Hiding mouth.

Touching ear.

Touching hair.

Pre-violence pose.

Uninterrogatable, "open on 8 sides".

Lip biting.

Dismissal.

Crossing.

Arrogant stance.

Carotid arteries.

Tensing shoulders.

Pursing lips.

"About to confess" chin support.

Antagonistic chin hold.

Body lean.

Hands to hair; "closing in".

Head-to-chest surrender.

Palms upward slump; pre-confession.

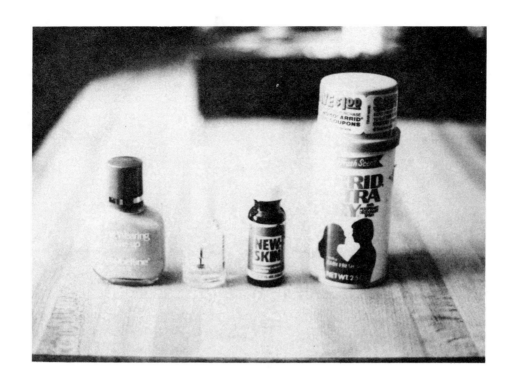

Skin tricks.

Works on some people...